Silent Whispers, Quiet Screams: Recovery is possible….

Not just in your dreams

Susanne Mills

© 2015 Susanne Mills
All rights reserved, including the right to reproduce this book or
any portions of it without the permission of the author

ISBN: 978-0-9908476-0-1
Published by Well YOUniversity, LLC

"CHAOS DEMANDS TO BE RECOGNIZED AND EXPERIENCED BEFORE IT CAN BE CONVERTED TO ORDER!"

Hakeem Bey

"Tell them about how you're never a whole person if you remain silent, because there's always that one little piece inside you that wants to be spoken out, and if you keep ignoring it, it gets madder and madder and hotter and hotter and if you don't speak it out, one day it will just up and punch you in the mouth from the inside."   Audre Lorde

To my heroes:
Steven Mills for being my first born and for always listening to me read.
Kevin Mills for being the Love of Jesus and my own personal "whatcha think" guy.

Thanks to:
My Mom and Sam for love cared.
My Dad, may she now Rest In Peace.
Larry for love learned, and being a part of my life for 40 years.
Anna O. for calming the noises and showing me peace
Jannae' A. for always pushing me forward
Jackie F. forever and for always friends
Chetta S. my supporter for all those morning glories, affirmations and designing my Invisible Happy Sombrero!
Sheri S. for wellness checks, unconditional love and reminding me to write it down!
Carol R. for all the support in getting this book out there
Jack H. for the self-love tactics and coping skills, you ROCK!
Lori E., Judy F. for soothing my many growing pains
Margaret and Shirla for taking that chance
Alfred, my friend through thick and thin
Elizabeth for showing me there is another side
All my colleagues that work so hard every day and make it all about the community we serve
All my friends at Riverbank for all the survival skills they have mastered & shared.
Everyone that showed me glimmers of light when I only saw darkness
And Bill C. without whom I would not have had the courage to share my transpose
For my self-worth, for finding its way back home

what is a poem?

the flight of an eagle,
the roar of the ocean,
the first beam of sunlight.
all of these,
seen through the eyes of a
poet,
start as an idea in his mind,
and become a poem from his
heart.
once an experience for him,
now only a memory
being shared.

window

from my upstairs window,
i stand above the world.
i see raindrops from top-side down
like beads on shiny pearls.

from my upstairs window,
i am so big and tall
because in my towering kingdom
i rise above them all.

chalk

white wonder in the hands
        of a mastermind
funny toy in the arms
        of a child

one writes
others learn
        sometimes

the child can
        playdrawcolor

why not?
        he is alive

i am   alone.

in the darkness
        of night
waiting to be relieved
        from my pain

i want to die
        in the dust
of this chalk

but first
        i wish to
        playdrawcolor
much like that child
        again

not just alive
        but free
free from the fear
        of death.

a sign

now I know
what it is like
to be trapped in
quicksand,
and for whatever reason,
i am too stupid or
too stubborn to stay
still.

so instead of
relaxing, waiting
to see if help
passes by, or
even calling out
for it,
i

sink

deeper.

i am afraid, no,
frantic,
so i
trudge

downward,
closer to my
demise
with my very own
aided assistance.

like the coyote,
with a dazed expression,
and a very small
please help!
sign,
very
quietly,

sinking.
beep! beep!

analysis-day 1
psych 101(clinical study)

depression is
miserable.
i sit here waiting,
desiring
those things in my life
which give it
purpose,
its reason and richness.

i go to the window
drawn by light or
curiosity (it is uncertain which)
expecting
to see things
from "normal"
visual perspectives.
instead i have unknowingly
picked up a kaleidoscope.
much to my surprise and
dismay,
twist-
the wire-locked over,
framed picture window,
intricate pattern
of obstruction and displacement
to the outside world.

oddly, initially, the design
is remarkably similar
to any, every
kaleidoscope i ever
toyed
with, unusual at this
moment, the hues
are unknown.

non-vibrant shades
of non-existent
color-
lacking vividness,

7   continued…..

                        variance,
                        obscure glare
                        colliding together,
                        in my scope.

                        making me realize,
                        that i want,
                        need,
                         my colors, patterns,
                        images back,
                        that unfiltered vision
                        once again…

analysis day 4
psych 101(clinical study)

peace has a price;
    everything does, i suppose.
peace of mind,
    now, here
can be difficult to achieve.
    its value
priceless.

oft times life
    feels like it will
fall to pieces.
    it goes around
full circle and then
    the pieces are
collected.

so it goes
    until the next occurrence.
different circumstances,
    same result: chaos.
similar process: collection,
    conclusion again
and again.

so it goes,
    controlling all
things
    in my life.
i want
    and need that
control.

build up,
    snowballing out
of control.
    no where to vent,
release the pressure,
    mind play
implosive.

silently shattering,
    mind collapsing,
shrapnel striking
    from within.

displacing, replacing logic,
    vision tunneled, unclear
focus.

pieces of brain
    lying on the floor
in my head,
    malfunctioning, misfiring,
falling to pieces
    like a collapsing house of cards,
jumbled.

clueless to how
    the turbulence
will be halted.
    unable to coagulate,
unable to solidify
    impulses, suddenly
severed.

searching for peace
    for myself and
my pieces.
    wanting to leave
with a full head,
    content to go
with function.

things will continue
    to be probed,
processed and controlled;
    however, when they spiral,
things that cannot be
    changed will be let
go.

let go
    for today
and dealt
with tomorrow.

a day
    of peace, not
pieces.

conversion of conversation

i met a homophobe today!

not my first,
nor my last,
how unfortunate.
luckily,
and this is being stated
somewhat reluctantly.

we had met before,
yet in actuality
we had not.

today,
on this day among days
of many
senseless,
thought-provoking moments,
we really conversed.

exchanged ideas,
Kris-crossed,
on one of many
networks of
intersecting,
conflicting,
seldom functioning
zones of
congested,

non-flowing,
non-communicative,
high volume traffic lanes
of language-carrying,

jams
of verbal banter.

swapping feelings
for ideas
or ideal
communication!

i stand
liking him
still.

now he knows
who i am,
where i stand.
what i hope
he will learn,
find
is acceptance.
no, something with
more grandeur,
tolerance,
fortitude,
awareness,
an open
mind.

spouse

the beauty and truth in a being lies in his soul,
something which can only be expressed when
he feels comfortable.
If and when you are, you speak openly,
free as the wind,
caring for no one, just yourself and the listener
as individuals.

joy

being happy is difficult
to imagine

simply because the lapse
of time
in between.
all these years
have been so very long.

i wait and wonder,
worry
if i will remember

how it feels?

Sole mate

if you run away
when you up and go
i want to take some space
to stop and let you know
i love you

even if my vision is not
yet clear
and my thoughts are
clouded through
my sights
my limitations
seem nearer
brighter too
with what you share
and show me
and teach me how
to feel
take a moment
pause
reflect
selfishly indulge your thoughts

you will see
that beaming inner glow
few will ever know
kindred soul
yours
a piece
of me
that i will keep
until
i

go

cerebral emancipation

Questioning
wondering
disconcerting
MIND　　　going
blank
　EYES　　　becoming
blind

Un-focusing
wandering
disconnecting
BODY　　　going
limp
HEART　　becoming
dead

Haggard
abused
defeated
VITALS　　checked
thump
SOUL　　　searched
Lifeless

ask me

ask me what
is wrong so that i
can say it aloud;
once and for
all to hear as it
screams from
here and bellows
out
of my clenched
fistbelly; once and
for all you will
hear why my screams
have been silent for
twenty eight years too
long.

me

i need to focus on me
learn to care about me
do things for me
selfish
happy
things.
if i can care about myself
then i can love you
i do for others
now
i feel i am no good
self-destructive
i must learn to leave
that behind me
so that I can survive

mom

bake cookies
cakes
pta
participate
patchwork
goose bumps
goose eggs
bruises
shopping trips
nuclear family
helping-hand
work ethic
moralistic
supportive
encouraging

seconds fly
past
player
                        fu m b l e s
passing
impersonate
replaceable
unable
no avail
no allowance
not allowed
you have
you are
you have
no more
chance
mom

fag

mom
no allowance
not
allowed.

cold as ice

blood
dripping
dripping

down
 it
r
a
n
overandunder
overandunder
cold
so cold.
the hand
    the hands
cold.
the eye
    the eyes
white.

cold
so cold
dripping
dripping

down
 it
r
a
n
overandunder
overandunder
red
    so red
        so cold

Soul mate

she can
touch my soul
without moving
a muscle

hear my disturbances
without a single
utterance

watch over me
from the
walls of her
heart

talk endlessly
forever
never
stopping to
wonder

how lucky
i feel

heart ache

intense
heavy
heated
      flickering
      flames of
passion

appeal

i
peel
a
way
peel
a
way
clothes
making
lovely
nude
mounds
of
soft
curvaceous
flesh

Magic WARD

magician
shuffles
 her cards

a cut
wave
the magic
wand and
begin

tricks
like,
i see a
i think it could be
you know what i'm saying?
you guys want to?

Her assistance
as she
shuffles
her audience
to respond

magical
illusion
delusion
as she
makes us
feel
like people
not
flowers
rabbits
doves
hats
or boards
not bored
just people
her assistants

magical
sorceress
shuffles
her cards,
a cut
wave
her magic
offerings

elaborate
stratagem
grand
delusion
enlightened
illusion
applause

AMAZON

       AMAZON tripped on
               a HOMOPHOBE today
       as she meandered
       across the floor

       at first, AMAZON
       was startled, caught off
       guard

takenaback.

       she felt like
        she needed
       someone
       to guide her

       LIFEguard
       her to safety

               thoughtlessworthlessknowledgelessplus,
                   she took a deep breath.

             AMAZON looked around.
     she called for help
     there was no one
      in sight

     feeling consumed,
     AMAZON went
         under

             panicthrashpaddlegurgle
     she came up for air

             AMAZON looked around
     she needed some help
     there was no one
     in sight

     feeling overwhelmed
     AMAZON went
         under

             quitpanicworthgurgleless

        she came up for air

            AMAZON looked around
          she searched for her helper
there was no one
in sight

feeling empowered
AMAZON got up

dustedherworthyassoff
she took a deep breath

        AMAZON and HOMOPHOBE
two control freaks
two JILLY goats
bangedtwotwoheads.

RESPECT
AMAZON called it
had her say
       and walked calmly   aw a y.

EDUCATED
the AMAZON BABE
spoke

I AM A WARRIOR!

life and love

i keep waiting for
life to improve
so that i will feel
free to love
again.

i dislike not knowing
how or where i am
going.
uncertainties of all future
aspects and prospects

emotional turmoil
troubles
self-loathing
insecurities

need to rekindle
burning
flames
of self-assurance
self-reliance

acceptance of
myself
discovery of
me

lunar

moon full
wolf howl
i hear his call
of the wild
and still is how i sit
hating myself
for allowing you
to touch
me

Hang(wo)man

rollingrolling
allaround
all
around
windingtick.
windingtick.
unraveling
each
 limb
inside
outside
upsidearound
body
engulfing
neck
forever
tight
outwitted
by
your
own
mind

movement in P sharp

limitedmovementlimited
access
watched
movementwatched
emotionswatched.
motions
e
ssential
frustrated
necessaryto
limitlife
threatening
movement
beltless
shoelaceless
aimless
face
in
my
reflection

Rape

Why is it easier to change
one's clothes,
than change one's thinking?
to change one's mind,
than all its reasoning.

Altering of perceptions,
        conceptions,
                condemnations.

Inflicted wounds foregoing,
self-inflicted scars concurrent.

Denial has its moments
outmoded by truths,
antecedents to realities.

Staring perpetrations in the face,
in his eye,
the man who taught this soul
that it could cry.

Penetrations violating deep
within this body,
        this mind,
               this soul.

Time has come,
it is so near
to shed some skin.

Find the energy,
the strength
to grow,
to change,
to live.

Life to its fullest
           (richest)
not with wealth,
but without guilt.

RAGE

What is it
that you feel?
that causes
you such rage?
such resentment?

HATE??

If I could
Rectify
Repair
the situation
the marriage
and know that you
would be happy
i think i would

DESPAIR??

If you were
older
would you
then understand
how sad?
uncomfortable
Vulnerable i am

It is not
an intellectual process
but rather an emotional
reaction
a response
something no longer
within my control

INNATE??

You make me
so uncomfortable
with myself
my desires
my visions

dreams clouded

obscured
by
thoughts of you

I miss
Your smile
Your laugh
mostly your compassion
your caring
your genuine concern
for my well-being

LOVE??

I do not like
the hate
the loathing
that you so often
feel
as you manipulate
aggravate
infuriate

I try to understand
i love
and hope
that one day
some day
you will love me
for who I am
who I have become
myself

Pt I-WarningSignalAndWhistlesAndBells,LIGHT

the greenengine
finds itself
in anawkward,
                    position
it is   shovedpushedforced,
intoa
              TUNNEL, it
could not
begin to imagine
and it
is   OVERWHELMING.
proportionate
to its' current vulnerabilities.

despite precautionary
measures,
there is no
resisting the
       FORCEand

the greentrain
goesinto
the darkness
un w illi ng ly
e v e r s o s l o w l y, it
speeds deep
into the
cavity of
unknown.
SHIT
it
is within confines
uncertain
restricted
from   wande rin   g
far off track
yet somehow
it feels
asif
its entiremachine is

descending somewhere.
it knows
it should
not go
familiarness.
it knows

it should
not go
déjà vu
déjà
vu.

there is
a loud NOISE
then SEVERAL.
it feels
asif
it may
        derail
try to
maintain CONTROL
slowdowndownshift
yetdownit

descends

the greenengine
sputters
to rectify
its predicament
a flash
is heard
knocking
ENGINE
it blinks
the weary
engine is
most reluctant to respond
the greentrain
steadies its
wheels against
the metal tracks
kindofsortof
downouttracks
the slightest
movement
couldsend
the whole
LOCO
inamotion

        falling.

Continued

                        the greenengine
                        CONTROLS
                        itself
                        veryveryslowly
                        finding the way   out
                        assisted by a
                        very bright
                                                LIGHT

Pt II-Coping on ENGINE 4-24

flash,
    the signal
    light   changes,
    ENGINEfollows
    the greenarrowgo.
    it finds
    its' way back
    to the track.

    the greentrain
    is slowleery.
    it goes to
    the very cold
    station at
    the rear
    of the hall.

    the signals
    are mixed,
    colorful,
    hard to
    distinguish.
    the intensity
    of light
    is metamorphic,
    LOUDER
    for all to
    hear.

    the signals
    continue
    as every
    colorfulvibrant
    shade of
    greenengines
    is guided
    into
    GRAND CENTRAL
    station.

    the crookedgreentrain
    slows down
trying to
    understand
    its direction.
SignalsAndWhistlesAndBells,
    LIGHT
     it sees the LIGHT

and does not

want to   go
to the directed,
final destination.

the crookedgreenengine
hesitates
idles,
uncertain.
it raises its arm
and signals
that it sees
the LIGHT
and arrives
as directed.

The crookedgreentrain
climbs out
of the greenLOCOmotive
of self-discovery,
self-recovery,
feeling queasy.

the greentrack
of Engine 4-24
has been l o n g,
twist
ed,
withchanges,

with delays
with a lie
uncertain
unclear
multioptional.

the greentrain
will
overlayover

and accelerate

s l o w l y,
timeprecious.

notanoption
it should be a
choice

Lincoln, Vermont

silently I scream
over and over again
in my dreams.

i can see you,
my biggest fear,
my worst nightmare.
when will you ever
go
away?

silently i screamed
repeatedly
in my visions.

i'll always see you,
delusions,
disillusions,
my mightiest obstacle
my internal opponent
you were smart, Lincoln
you were strong, Lincoln
you were wrong, Lincoln.

go away--
forever. for i will
no longer scream
silently…
ever.
my screams
will be heard.

may 7(+3)

a cart rolls
rollsalongit
shakes.
tires rattle
withthe
steady beat
of a metronome.
the wooden slats
creakcrackle
shifting weight.
crates.
i, the ox
stand
tall
proudly.
Trying to
appear
proud
at least
faultless

silent
clumsy ox.
pullingalong
my
cart.
mine
on wheels.
spinning around.
spinning past.
spinning present.

roundandround.
lifefullcircle.
sweet breath.
putrid bile
sealed inside

crate
stacked
up onexto
another
crate.
boxes
of
litter
a
ture.
materials
im
material
articles.
artifacts
worn
over.
walked
over.
pictures.
smells.
 touches.
shades.
developed
stenches.
grappling.
omni
present.
stop.
this.
fucking.
cart.
shoot.
it.
dead.
OXY
moron

enlightenment marches in (3-1-98)

in captivity the girl shivers,
the humidity reeks,
fear dictates every move
she makes.

his hollowness,
strategically placed in stone,
holding the balance between
flesh and BONE,
barricading her from escape.
nightmares growing.

Finally the MASS reaches its
HEIGHT and whispers bitterness
inside, licking at her
eversoslightly.

with power and strength he
ravages on,
tearing horrifically against her,
his animalism met, he breaks
and hesitates
only to begin AGAIN.
a powerful struggle
that only takes 34 years,
89 days,
and one special $100.00 hour,
for her to break-free
from his hold, to realize,
that it was not her fault.

kudos, Judy!!

ebb

warm rays of passion stream down and heat my shoulders
raising the pulse of my heart
creating a lovely deep breath that seeps down into my belly
and helps me relax.
as i sit totally at peace with the world
i realize
that if it weren't for your spirit
i would be missing a very important part
of my soul

pupils

    deep and rich
flavored
chocolate
melting on a warm day
eversoslowly.

dark and absorbent,
novelistic,
unfolding with suspensesurprise,
interwoven.

bright and playful
dancers
joyous with
dimpled smiles.

power source,
a switch that ignites,
glancing,
flickering, sparkleflash.

increase the rhythm,
increase the pulse.
palpitations of joy
tickling my heart
with only your eyes.

On Guard

I feel his whisper.
I see the sounds.
I burn my body.
It feels so amazingly decorous,
Genuine.
It is such an incredible rush.
MY power
MY feeling
Total control
Yet so entirely out of control.
Turmoil
Inner-agitation
Self-hatred
Delusional Disorder
Absolutely no order
No rhyme…
Just reason.
Get rid of the inner pain
By inducing more pain
To this external source
With My blade
In My blood
Cold steel
And I feel the stab
Of quick discernment,
So I play
Acting outward
Dying inward
Sitting ashamed.
How could I do this again?

unconditional love

you should have put a gun to your head
and blew your brains out
are the words my loving son
said to me in anger.
it would have made life easier
life would have been better,
instead of what you have done.

how do you look into aching teenage eyes
and say, oh yeah, i almost did.
after all; he's just a kid.
wouldn't life be simple
if you could speak the truth,
if you didn't have to consider
the impressionableness of youth.

you should have put a gun to your head
and blew your brains out.
loving mom,
hateful son,
ranting angst,
no picture perfect dream here.

then he went his way
as if all were normal
how do you explain that you can't explain,
that you should not have to explain
everything.
normal,
     nothing further from the truth.

you should have put a gun to your head
and blew your brains out.
many days I want to-
a hard thing to fight
for a life when you don't know
if what you're doing is right.
BANG!
you're alive,
time to survive.

unconditional love (revisited)

with massive talons he tears through her flesh,
seizing the muscle of her heart,
squeezing, unbearably until he draws the fight
out of its rhythm,
and she stands with no energy or resistance.

he holds tight with a grip that will not let go,
lasting a week until she is wounded enough
to no longer submit to his violent hold.
with delicate grace she works at her diction;
well rehearsed, it resonates in triumphant harmony.

encircling the wound, she wraps a chord around
the vessels,
prying the muscle free from his clawing grip,
with lyrics so clear and unobstructed,
he is astounded and stands back, gawking.

wings slowly envelop her arms.
in freedom she soars overhead, singing victoriously,
unafraid of reoccurring injury
and having made a glorious discovery:
motherhood sails to full recovery.

unhappy

drop
      ping

down
 b
 e
 l
 o
 w

buried

deep
within
skin
cells
layers

negative
feelings
docked
in
harbors
like
ships
wrecked.

Pick Three

i found a lamp,
a tattered,
dull,
slightly golden
lamp.

rub three wishes.
three magic
wishes
is what was
wished for
and that was one.

my second was to
stand straight, and
i was erected, my hunch
nullified.
straight like the
steel beams in a
toy construction set.

my third and last
heartfelt, most
desirous of all.
anticipation and
i salivate immensely
at the very
slight possibility
of completely laughable
totally silly
happiness.

joyfulness
giddiness, and
 glee.

i wished for
happiness
many years ago…
and i believed it had
come true, and perhaps

it did, for a while.

i do not know.
misery is recognizable.
familiar.
i want it
clearly
marked
this time
around.

mirror,
mirror,
on the wall,
bring me selfish
elation
once
and
for
all.

reflection

having fondled death
with my own
hand
of fate

and surviving Reaper's
grim tug

i now reflect on
life with a new
out look.
just knowing it will
get better
might be
enough

Sand

light appears and the hourglass is turned,
the dropped, the past
the dropping, the present
growing old,

the remaining,

what yet

will

come.

some,

fromtimetotime
turn the hourglass on its side,
spending today in yesterday,
never touching their tomorrows.

So I Pray

Now I lay me down to sleep
No need to pray
No soul to keep
in my head
a wooden box
the door is closed

From the distance
a light flickers
there is a knock
on the lid
I come out
for now

to stay
to battle
to win
i hope

the visitors

i walk silently down the beach,
in anticipation of meeting new friends,
morning--
alas.
the sun rises to wake them.
they toss,
and turn,
then arise.
oh, how they glisten
in the morning light.
they rush in,
shake my hand
as if to welcome me
to their seaside home.
then,
inaninstant
they
lower
    t   heir heads and vanish
                      beneath
                                their Cape.

the Villain toes
he tugs,
trying to take them
                away.
despite their natural bondage
they escape
againandagain,
change faces each time
in an effort to disguise themselves.

good-bye
they Wave,
and off they go
perhaps i will visit
tomorrow.

S.O.S.
(swim or sink)

                mping,
i'm used to   ju
up
      and
              down,
roundandaround,
on that little spot
(patch) of earth
that is
(was) my life…
the earth t r e m b l e d,
and s h o o k
until my patch
(spot) opened
(cracked) beneath
my feet and i
kind of
tee
      tered.

i found what used
to be my life
(past) in a pool
of liquid.
am i falling?
am i drowning? i am
definitely

          sinking.

the liquid is thick
(murky) and all my
usual survival
(swimming) techniques
falter. my effort
(less)ness is in vain.

i am searching for a
life jacket, life-
line, something to help
support me. wanting

to overcome this

miserable
(deplorable) state of
existence. every part
of me is vulnerable.
nothing seems
(sur)passable.

wanting to hold on,
wanting to l e t   go

seek and hyde

I feel so lonely
like Cousin
It.
I am
It. as you hide
yourself so well
from everything, i
keep searching for,
hoping and waiting
until you allow
yourself to be
found. along the
way i keep finding
wonderful others--
friends that want to
play, and so I do,
while in my heart
i dream, still
needing to find
my friend that
hides so deeply.
 i keep searching when
you are again
ready to come
out come
out where
ever
you are. i will
be ready
to play without
the games
of the mind

Sandpit

face down pushedeepin
the sand,
my face learned
as my ass burned
what men did
to make babies for
fun.
only the fun was
not there,
just the dumb baby
with the burning bum
trying frantically
to twitch her way
    out
     from
    under
     the hunter
until she wriggled
out of her shell
and floated safely
overhead, sobbing,
until it was over.
sinking down a second
time thinking i'd get
up, he spoke in
frightening whispers
and decided to delve inward
    again.
   when I finally
floated

     back,
     i lay
     motionless
      for longer
than i want to remember.
finally shuffling off
never to look at my world

  the same way again.

target practice

like a weapon, he discharges his chamber,
preying on tiny targets
which she has set out for him.
nonchalantly scattered about, unsuspecting,
two shots, one bullet.
bulls-eye, it feels as his casing thrusts forward,
ripping at its' flesh with intense pain and consequence,
while she watches, unknowingly, doing nothing,
giggling in his presence.

why did she bring this weapon?
teasing with him while it suffers, frightened,
why does she treasure him so?
his wicked craftsmanship creeps upon the offspring.
targets left in solitude to roam without guidance,
unsecured enclosure that offers no protection,
little targets torn apart forever,
circular specks of blood-red childhood dying,
swaying in the wind like bludgeoned f r a g me n t s,
upsidedownside it hangs.

powerless victim wanting to scream,
silent in its own fear,
never feeling safe in its' own mind.
bleeding target forever afraid, left dangling by a thread,
peeled like an onion, layer after layer, without a tear.
he sucks it up like a vulture,
whispering in its' ear,
fearing for Her life
left behind like an
offering

the art of therapy

i love art.
i admire my teacher
as she does her work,
guides me,
into perceptions
that gradually
brighten
my world.

tuitioned by
gently
tracing trails
of events
gone   array.
stringently making
every effort not to
venture off course.

scholastically
sketching shades,
varying the intensity,
and levels of
intimacy,
swirling the words
to create
filtered shadows.

directing by,
drawing out
ideas
and feelings
that differ
in color, and lineage
horizontally bright,
vertical, intensely, difficult.

erudition through
painting
with her words
of brilliance and

intelligence through
wisdom gained,
and shared,
in vivid pigmentation.

standing distanced
to behold
easel cradled
masterpiece.
i love art. i admire my instructor
as she processes,
without judgment.

curvilinear passage
into solar
eclipse, embracing
lunar matter,
evolving through
a pinhole
into a paradigm,
within my mind.

expression

i grasp the red crayon,
and try to sketch an apple.
instead, i make a simplistic
sphere with a stem
and two leaves.

i concentrate and select
a lovely light blue sword,
and with it i begin to strike
my attack
on the rich
rolling water
waving its arms to tease
the many grains of sand
as they evaporate into the
dying brown of the desert.

i envision a brilliant purple
butterfly,
fluttering its wings freely.
as i envelop it with
vibrant shades, i discover
that what i have illustrated
is a gray, fuzzy, common,
light bulb-chasing insect,
and thus it continues
until i try each one.
only to find out that my pigment
has changed, irreversibly.
my taste buds have dulled.
my future has washed away.

sure it is bold,
certainly it is dark.
there is no clearer way
for me to illustrate
just how this feels
to want to be erased.

am i entitled to happiness?

i am becoming educated in happiness…
a feeling that i do not remember.
it is an awesome effortless expression
relaxing and calm.
i am entirely envious of others' laughter…
i need to claim my own.

screamachine

up and down i ride,
wanting someone to notice
that i am trapped on
this amusement
too afraid to scream
aloud, for fear of being discovered
without a ticket.
my brain no longer fits
insidemyhead.
only a portion
is skulled in tact.
the bulk has
fallen   out,
in p i e c e s .
one such piece sits on my lap
with a white cotton napkin
          underneath
it is protected by my meds
and is carefully carted
to and fro in my hands.
it usually stays with me,
though not completely
as before.
some smaller pieces are shoved
inmypockets
like spare change,
different sizes and densities,
some shiny, others worn.
my most important lobe
is placed inside my shoe
to hide it away-
to keep it safe,
secret,
unreachable,
unsalvageable,
the thoughts and words washed off
       in perspirous dramatic foot s t e p s.
              w i d e   strides,
shortsteps.

no one will notice me
as I walk away from here.

Shrink-wrap

for years, I carefully tucked away necessary emotion,
wrapping each investment separately--
some taped with bubble wrap,
others raw, yet carefully surrounded by foam peanuts
still more wrapped loosely in newspaper.
the infectious being treated as sacred
placed on foam sheets and wrapped softly,
then tucked in Styrofoam boxes
    and quickly shrink-wrapped to hold them in forbidden suspension.
swallowed packages that were allowed to sit and fester,
and life was good, or at least okay
as I play-acted my way through it.

until one unforgettable day,
or a series of horrible ones,
I simply won't allow myself to remember which,
I found myself standing on my head, obsessing.
the packages began dropping from my gut and into my throat
like gifts pouring down the chimney on Christmas morning--
and I choked,
more like gagged.
I didn't asked for these presents,
nor was I ready for what they held inside,
so I pushed them back to that comfortable spot
and they boomeranged toward me.
they came in massive quantities,
too quickly to categorize.

what do I do now?
which one do I pick up first?
sounds are surrounding me that I hardly recognize.
I'm screaming, but it is very surreal.
it came from one of those packages, didn't it?
I am not responsible, am I?
like uninvited guests that won't go home,
they sit and chortle at me.
I have suddenly become a birthday party clown
who attempts to juggle without knowing how.
hoping to improve, yet destined to struggle through the interim
in an uncomfortable costume and floppy shoes,
biting at my painted lip to hide my anxiety.

I need to return my circus pass
and sit down with my inner child
to celebrate the discovery of these treasures.
rip each package open carefully and play with the contents.
put them to use
and learn what they can offer me.
a forty-year-old child learning how to hold
a masterfully crafted butterfly with thread antennas,
and a magnificent purple hue
without the foam sheet wrapper,
without the Styrofoam box,
without the shrink-wrap cocoon-
just the raw emotion of human anger
and not breaking under the pressure.

SOARING

I stand on a cliff,
The same one I have always wanted to jump off of,
And I look around.

I see that it has always been a mountain peak,
A summit with only gradual inclines,
Not gnarled peaks.

As I stand,
I realize that I am not alone.
I have a repertoire of constructed components,
Making up an unfashionable, yet serviceable glider, of sorts.

It offers broad wings.
A strap in harness,
And a runty engine.

Time to pull the motor's cord,
And fly in my machine.

Guided by the winds of fate,
Supported by my mind,
With all its' strength and knowledge,
 It takes off with a staunchly launch.

No longer leery or surveying the world astern,
Drifting out, among the clouds,
Without despair.

Facing emotion,
Encountering confrontation,
Challenging interactions,
Or at least expediting their departures.

Unafraid of what might be arriving,
Fearless, as I view my new world
With landing gear out
And a parachute strap in hand.

Screening

i SCIPped into the woods

once upon a time,

on a dark and cloudy night.

i came in for a cleansing of sorts,
in both mind and soul.
i found a mighty switch to hold,
discovered a gnarled rod,
its' lengthy curl bent high above.
give me that branch,
with a white flag,
to wave far and wide.
not bottling things up like before,
to hold deep down inside,
not beating myself up.
or thinking of suicide.
i have been able
to sound this alarm,
to hoist up that white flag inside my head,
and wave it high in the sky.
to surrender and ask for help from friends,
knowing they will always be there.
remembering those tools are always with me
standing at my side.
watch the prisoners i take
as I lash out at the world for the very first time,
do not misdirect my anger,
for this is only my start.
many still lie in this meadow
wounded deep in the heart.
no need to strike between their eyes
I want them to see clearly,
that we all ache deep down inside.
with all His good graces,
may we all stand and unite,
to form a bonded community
as we all battle for a better life.

Good Night, Sweet Nurse

Kind and sweet,
Kept so neat,
Strength with caring,
Wisdom and sharing…
Elasticwoman

Stretching in ten directions,
Multi-tasking with affection,
Lots of time spent talking,
Little time for leisure walking…
Elasticwoman

No ego trip,
Hands on hips,
Lovely lady of care,
Always ready to share…
Elasticwoman

Eat and run,
Lots of fun,
Always ready to help,
Compassion heart-felt
Elasticwoman

discharged

The time has arrived,
The day is mine,
Adaptations.

Life is still young,
Challenges to come,
Adaptations.

Take that first step,
With no regrets,
Adaptations.

Afraid to unlock,
Please do not let me stop,
Adaptations.

Time to go,
Now I know,
Adaptations.

Time to fly,
One more time,
Adaptation.

Vacation in Lourdes

I took a journey today,
An empowering and wondrous trip
I visited the Lord today,
With guidance and compassion.

I traveled my soul today.
I had several people by my side
That I will always keep with me.
We searched our past today
With forgiveness and understanding.

We felt your presence today
As we faced our current fears.
I listened as she sang today,
Escaping her past.

We hit a milestone today
As we learned to accept and let go
We abandoned our shadows today,
So now we can soar.

Someday, we will fly, oh Lord,
Like butterflies escaping a cocoon.
We found a beauty today
Lying deep within our spirits.

A monarch was born today,
Colored with many different hues.
I tried to flutter today
And found my wings tattered and torn.

So now we pray today
To the Glorious and Almighty.
We found a source today
To help lessen the pain

We learned to love ourselves today
As we escaped the abyss
I found myself today
And with that I will not miss.

Soul Sister

Her kindness is encompassing,
Her spirituality divine,
I am so glad to have found
That dear, dear soul inside

Through her lovely spirit,
Through those rich brown eyes,
I was able to find
A very special power
That shall always be mine

For I was but a prisoner,
Being eaten up alive.
Now I stand in wisdom
My spirit no longer hides
It guides me to the light

What a lovely beauty
With a jewelry box of gold
A heart filled with guidance
An essence ever so bold

Of this grand transition,
From which I shall never part,
I will always remember
Her magnificent heart.

Once Upon A Life Partner

Your precious words are so lovely to hear,
They make me smile and glisten.
My spirit seems lifted by your thoughts
To a wonderfully special place
That I have never been to before

You make me forget that I am lonely.
      I cannot wait to hear your voice on the phone,
To see your face again,
Gaze deep into those eyes.
I can't wait to smile with you…
Laugh with you,

Stand by your side.
 I want to hold you and never let go.
 I need you to know
That I love you so.

You excite me,
Ignite my spirit from my soul
You make me feel beautiful,
I am loving it so.

I yearn to kiss you,
Touch your face
Please be strong in life
As you stand within my space.

I do not want our love to stop.
I just will not let go.
Be by my side forever
As we live and love and grow.

cerebral emancipation

Questioning
wondering
disconcerting
MIND   going
blank.
EYES   becoming
blind

Un-focusing
wandering
disconnecting
BODY   going
limp
HEART   becoming
dead

Haggard
abused
defeated
VITALS   checked
thump.
SOUL   searched
Lifeless

Yet still
Alive

Hello, my name is Susan

Hello, my name is Susan…
I'm sick; will you help me?
Such an intrusive request,
Especially difficult to get up and announce,
Denounce.

As I shook those hands
Looked deep into wounded faces,
Two of those faces
Actually smiled at me.
I actually found myself smiling back at them.

It just happened.
It was eerie.
I never would have predicted it.
Here I was depressed as all hell,
Suicidal ideations racing,
Self-mutilation happening
In very psychotic ways

Yet here I was able to smile.
It opened the door to healing.

There is a long road ahead of me,
Many demons to finally face
I do not even know yet
If I can find strength to face them

I will try, however,
Because now I know
That we all suffer something
Many functioning better than others

Still, I might get the chance
To help myself
Tread water a little harder
Maybe even swim a lap

Thanks to one tough guy
With a soft heart
Who lives in the world
 That "Jack" built

The beanstalk and Jack

I met a man-
Strong and mighty,
Who had once climbed a beanstalk,
He spent his time taking people
On adventures of that stalk

Together they would climb steadily toward the sky,
To find the place where the giants hide.
With his guidance,
And sensitivity,
They slowly reached the top.

At his castle
 High in the sky,
The battled their mighty monsters,
Some together,
Others separately,
But battle they did!!

And continued this process…
Until the war was won

And though their struggles may continue,
And their conflicts may be fierce,
The stories of Jack and the Beanstalk,
Will always serve as weapons
As we travel into oblivion

Horticulture

If I could be any flower
A rose I'd choose to be

I would keep my thorns upon my stem
To represent my steps on this path to knowledge

I would grow more beautiful and full
My vulnerabilities revealed to help me feel alive

I'd drink a little water
Some sugar and TLC

I will continue to grow forever
Until I finally become a tree.

Choo-Choo Charlie and the Engineer

I once met a man who was brilliant,
Although I did not know it at the time
He was very ill and it was intense to watch him struggle,
Yet slowly he fought the difficulties.
Progressively he tamed the beast,
Regaining his strength and radiance.
Soon he began to blossom,
Coming through with glamour and with grace.
I will always remember
That I made a friend in this place.

from bruiser

we put our faith in ourselves
      so that our health may be directed
            on a positive course,
        knowing all along that we walk with God
          we travel together.
     forever but a phone call away…
              with kisses on one another's boo boos.

friendship

today I lost a buddy
tomorrow I'll have a lifetime friend
forbidden secrets only we can share
of how we have grown
with how much we have learned
we can now stand together
hold each other's hand
lean on one another's shoulder
know we'll always have support
forever together
in pain and in glory.

Recovery Inc.-Mental Health Unit

i feel my growth has been tremendous,
and still i am not through.
it has taken all of my will
to stand here strong and tall.
yet I will always know,
that I did not get there on my own.
it took tools,
i used steps,
in storing these weapons of self-defense.
through it all
the entire way
i walked in the hands of friends.
as i travel forward,
if i should start to fall back,
i can struggle through the storms.
yet keep in mind,
i will always know
there will forever be,
a special place for me to grow
should i ever need to go.

Workshop

I am a work in progress,
With little nails and pegs
Tapped firmly into place.
Thanks to a very strong and understanding face.

I am forever growing,
I hope to always climb
In an upward motion
With her words of wisdom pushing from behind.

My equivalent

My arms are held wide-open
I do not want it to stop
This feeling I am finding
This love within my heart

I've searched all of my life,
For an equal partner and friend
Standing side by side
Like minds and like-spirited

I want the whole world to know
Just how much I care
And each passing moment
Is one I want to share!

Mr. Sandman

He walks the halls at night,
Checking on our safety,
Dropping sand in our eyes,
And quietly watches over us.

A blanket to tuck us in
If ever we are chilled,
With his warmth, compassion and caring,

He quietly approaches
And gently awakens us from our slumber
To carefully check vitals
And not disturb us from our dreams.

Crazy love

a constant struggle
within,
to achieve,
to perceive,
a state,
a constant state
(never)
of some level
on some level
or plane,
feeling
a constant feeling,
(rarely)
with someone
without someone
love
a constant love,
(sometimes)
the one
and only
consistency
a search
deep within
the soul
that microscopic
(probably smaller)
speck
of nothingness
that harbors
everything.
the deepest
darkest
part of
toto
the ugliest
most vile,
most remarkable,
gorgeous
aspects.
proper feeding,
nurturing,
probing,
to surface.
mystical components
function
as you

fa
  ll
wonderfully
in
love.

Super Powers

I now possess super powers.
New untapped energy I am finding within.
I slowly strap them to my utility belt
To keep forever at my disposal

And when I need to reach them,
No need to run and hide.
For all I need to hold them,
Is to reach deep down inside.

linda

this is my aunt, linda,
was what I had to say
when someone met my dad.
i was barely thirteen--
he should have known better
than to show me his naked breasts
and picture upon picture
of his body in masquerade.
only it wasn't a party
or a freaking game.
it was dad,
only it was not
my dad…

not any longer.
it was the Woman that swallowed him whole,
only he was no longer
whole…
or was he?
I stood staring at two rather large breasts
larger than what was growing on my own little chest
as I too transitioned into
Womanhood.
me and my dad
who was no more
dad,
just an aunt with his new
niece,
a niece that did not know
how not to change
all the mutations that were going on in
my own teenage mind
as I began to cycle month after month
as a woman for the first time.

ironically,
and I state that very reluctantly,
i later in life met a man
who never cycled this
carnivorous red trail
that I had blazed
with my bulging belly
and those horrible
growing pains…
cramps,
as I had
pains…agony.
evolving into a woman who loves women.

it was a lesbian support group
which two kids later I
kindofsortof needed.
a solid source of comfort,
or so I thought.
it was there I met

a group of womyn
who loved women
and there stood Karla larger than life
as Karl prepared for his surgery.
Stage two
so that he could also become
the official Tran-sexed
lesbian

how did that happen?
i briefly contemplated.
did he still love women?
unchanged?
like linda ?
a lesbian?

i had a major metamorphosis
into that teenager again
at thirtysomething
who was as scared as could be
watching those blossoming bosoms

and not wanting to change
into my dad
in front of my children's eyes.
so I deduced
that they would be better off
not knowing my own confusions
or me

and my secret identity.
dead, better off dead.
so I lived for a while
dead

they knew…
they had the misfortune of being told
by their very own mother.
so I cried
and kept crying…
year after year
in morbid cogneto
until I finally accepted that I too had a right

to live exhaling…
with the love of my life
standing beside me
out and about
loud and queer,
still wishing dad
had never opened his shirt to me
and not wanting to do
similar injury to my two young men
while knowing damage is still being done
and I'm unable do a damn thing to
stop
it,

if I want to inhale
all that sacred air…
called life
to which I somehow feel entitled to.

i just wish it didn't hurt so much
cause I miss my kids.
and I want them to one day say
when they meet someone they know
this is my Mom…
and mean it.

My Life

She lights my world with her smile,
She lifts my spirit with her voice,
She makes my day with that style,
I pick her over all by choice.
My dear partner that I adore,
Has such unique and genuine allure,
I can't wait to hold her near,
My sweet, my darling, my dear,
Love so special at this time,
You make my life worthwhile and fine,
May you be blessed with all the happiness you give me.
You keep my mind willful and filled with glee.

Once Upon a Value

Today I take your hand,
To hold in mine forever
Like two little girls holding hands
On the playground,
I stand enchanted.

A modern day fairy princess,
With her Princess Charming.
Two women together
in a rainbow of color,
Encircled in gold,
Committed to a self-induced state of Euphoria.

You are my blessing,
My best friend,
My partner,
My mate.

May we slowly build our castle,
Live happily within its walls,
Stand side by side,
As we soar beyond the sky

Hearts held high!

My J's

I'm in love with Wonder Woman,
And it is a gift of delight
It feels so absolutely perfect,
Yet despite all my might,
I can't help but wonder
What makes love so special?
This time around

I have fallen in love with Wonder Woman,
And it is the feeling of pure elation.
It can't help but be noticed,
This meeting of the minds
We want to let the world know
That we are hopelessly, happily, whole-heartedly,
Entirely, wonderfully, madly in love

My miraculous Wonder Woman,
With her new special powers,
Has stumbled across my mentor,
And is surrounded by his aromatic flowers,
Possessing superlative beauty,
And fantastic range
I can't help but notice
Her wonderful change.

Wonder Woman is an individual;
She is so unique,
Encompassed by wisdom
That is ever so sweet
Thanks for growing stronger
And standing by so boldly
I cannot wait until she holds me,
To be touched by her new energy.

Again thanks to Jack
For giving me my friend back.
Now comes the hard part
As she tackles her nemesis
That is keeping her under attack.

We now see her stronger
With powers abundant.
I know she'll survive empowered
By added strength and new skills.
I love her so much;
Thank you both for the thrills.

dribble

the words came dribbling out of her mouth,
very quickly and confounded.
it created a mélange of melodrama,
more vehemently than she could imagine possible.
times were awesome,
life was divine,
and here comes this drool of disapproval…
infectious,
demoralizing,
lethal.
pummeling into the lobes of emotion,
all reasoning impinging on indifference--
it impacted with potency,
domination,
vigor,
brute strength,
and POW it rebounded sky-high,
then traveled downward again
creating a massive collision
as the shit hit the fan
and the ball banged into my head.
advantage…visitor.

it traveled upward,
attempting to play with my psyche.
stability no longer protected,
uncertainty   protruding,
no longer sacred.
chafed and tattered,
using all my resources,
taxing all angles
until the dribble
was put into play.
the shot was attempted
from outside the line.
three points.
score.
advantage--home.

time out.
the ball was fouled;
home team takes possession.
.coach rehearses the play.
the ball is in our court.
the call was clear.
its resonance rang out

with assurance and deftness,
ingenuity and expertise.
the final minutes counting down.

the players became disheartened.
the ball travels up and down.
I kept control,
saw the opening,
took the shot.
I could almost see the crowd on their feet
slam dunk

we had won the game.
only it was not a game.
it was life,
our life.
we had taken control.
the clocked ticked out the final seconds.
we stood victorious,
tainted,
yet poised.
we will survive,
be ready for the next round.
this took every ounce of effort
every spec of self-discipline
tapped our inherent resources,
tested our courage,
our fortitude.
somehow we emerged
empowered,
reassured
that whatever we want
we can achieve
with teamwork,
for we are the champions
of our own little world.

Silent Night

As I sat in church
On that Christmas Eve
Of the year 2005
At their candlelight service,

I held my candle
With its little plastic handle
I picked nervously at the wick,
Anticipating the rejoicing,
Of the singing of Silent Night.

With the start of Christmas
In all its glory,
I was quite somber
As I picked at that tiny wick.

I sat there thinking I had gotten a dud
I hoped it would light
As that flame would later pass around
In the sharing of the holy light

I sat there knowing
That somehow it would work
God had the power
He would give me his light.

He would give me the pleasure
On this glorious night
My eyes would tear,
I would then know that it was Christmas.

The story of the birth of Christ was told
The people around me sang
I sat there listening,
Enveloping,
Yet I did not sing.

I wasn't feeling it,
Yet part of me was experiencing great joy,
The service drew to a close.

The flame came from a single candle,
To another and another.

It went throughout the entire church.

The lights went down

At the back of the church
Where I had been seated.

I now stood.
I tried to light my candle
With the assistance of fellow worshiper.
I held my little wick
Close to her flame,
Success!

I moved back to my place.
My candle went out,
So I tried to light it again
It went out.

Yet the spirit of Christ was with me
As my partner stood next to me.
Holding her burning candle,
Aided by a stranger.

She shared her flame with me;
I took my time
I let the wax to burn
It held light.

Then it went out again,
So I gave up.
The song was starting;
Hundreds of flames burned brightly.

The music rang out
I stood there
I sang
With my unlit candle held tightly in my hand.

Silent Night,
Holy Night,
All is calm,
All is bright

Sleep in Heavenly Peace.

In my shadowed-darkened world,
Surrounded by burning flames,
I stood with nothing
Save the exception
Of that unlit candle,
Wondering why this was happening.

I was to find out on Christmas morn
That my dad passed
Christmas Eve.

About the same time
I had been trying,
Failing,
To light that candle

The divine symbol
Of that candle
Trying to stay lit
With my Dad's spirit
Standing by my side,
Blowing it out.

I was meant to sing in the dark
That Christmas Eve
As my father departed his life,
Then soared into eternity.

Silent Night,
Holy Night,
All is calm,
All is bright.

Sleep in Heavenly Peace, Dad,
Sleep in Heavenly Peace.

Everlasting Glance

Staring into those eyes of green,
Most beautiful face I have ever seen.
Flecks of brown dance around,
Making your gaze unique and profound.
Entwining deeply within our souls
Your piercing glance makes me whole.
You make me delighted that we have the time
To stroll gaily into our minds,
To explore the sensation of true romance,
Knowing we will give our love a chance.
The result is stupendous, beyond expectation.
Your eyes they twinkle and give me palpitations
Exploring our spirits and hearts divine.
Please look my way just one more time.
 I will return your ever-so-welcoming stare
To let you know I will always care.

smirk

She smiles and makes me laugh
She looks into my eyes and makes me wonder
About the many possibilities…
About the future…
About life…

Muscles

I've been aroused
To be a stronger person
By the woman that I love
Life has become exciting
Love has become enticing.

I want to be better
In how I respond,
How I carry myself,
How I react to others,
In the way that I love.

I need to take time to treat
Countless others with respect,
Use wisdom gained
To assist woman and man-kind,
In the same devotion I feel.

In my life,
Toward my partner,
For myself,
With happiness,
Toward new acquaintances.

With old friends,
In the workplace,
In the world.
It is such an inspiring feeling,
So liberating.

Integral,
Sensation of vigor,
Resourcefulness,
Emotions magnificent,
Passions flowing.

Sluiced,
Drained,
Running off,
Overflow of powerful
Susceptibilities.

Naked,
Evacuated,
Exhausted,
Invigorated…healthy and strong.

Play

I want to play with you.
Take a walk in the rain.
Climb a big tree and
Watch from above as others stroll by
Unaware of our hidden presence
To run in the wind with you,
Or play in the sun
Building castles in the sand

I would like to hold hands my friend.
Laugh out loud.
Have someone to tell all of my secrets to.
Who will love me despite my flaws
A friend to keep me safe
In your soft and tender arms
Someone with a heart of gold and.
The spirit of a lion

A body to hold so close
To help me through my fears
    Someone who will sing to me when I am afraid
To shade me from the heat
Someone exactly like you
Who makes my heart skip a beat

RESPITE

Crisis House counselors taught me to explore
That part of me I never knew before.
I only knew I didn't want to live,
Yet Crisis House staff helped me to learn to forgive.
Stable medication two times a day
It made me want to stick around and play.

A part of me has always wanted to die;
At Crisis House they taught me that I could try
To live life to the fullest extent
Taught me spirituality to make my heart content,
Gave me a roof over my head,
Three square meals, and a comfy bed.

Peer counselors and so much more.
Supervisors up one floor,
Drop-ins come in and then they go.
It's open house watch a show
Old Crisis House teaches you to let life flow
Give it direction
let it go

They taught me coping tools so I could grow.
Housing I am now proud to show-
I don't even stop to ask God why
Cause Crisis House has helped me fly.
Now all I do is reach my arm up high-
And I can easily touch the highest star in the sky

La La Land

I took a winter night's trip
Into the realm of La La Land
It began in sweet conversation
And ended in those lovely lips

Now we are separated,
Not by anger or distress,
Just a quick readjustment;
    Soon we will stand back together, reunited.

Let us expedite the process
With a little love and sharing.
Keep us well and keep us strong,
 So that we can play again, in our great love

Needing conjugal attention,
In areas I cannot mention.
Let us start in the sharing;
Give us time for love and caring.

I cannot wait until you are free,
Cause then it will be just you and me
With the help of a little fairy dust
And a lot of sheer caring

Let us revisit La La Land;
In with the likes of Foreverandeverland
A wonderful excursion
Into our first kiss…

This second time around!

The Man that Can

My life was spent going around in circles.
The music played and I turned the crank.
It was not really working
as the rubber band circle twisted more taunt.
Out popped a jack
from a sturdy metal box.
He stood noble.

I do not know what was done,
but something clicked,
a slight synapse,
a spark shot out,
glue still hot off the presses.
It worked
all the pieces finally fit.

I do not know what it was,
but it was exerting ideas;
thoughts were like crystal;
meditation was boisterous;
ideas were encompassing;
so I jumped
through verbal hoops.

Repetitious interruptions
foreign exchange
unusual suspects
alibis
unidentified flying objections
inhalations
famous last words.

So I keep it simple;
reflect,
address each premise,
and slowly unfold my blanket.
Foundation still not complete,
ready-poured and hardening, though.
and I take another breath

hearing his voice.
Relax, says the jack.
Divine inspiration
respiration gradually accomplished,
so we talk as I draw in
uneasy, yet willing to search
for a preferable existence.

Friendly Fire

My life snowballed
like an avalanche
sliding down the mountainside.
It gained momentum
and grew as it rolled
layer to layer
overontopof
instead of falling.
It slid
definitely outward
like projectile vomit at 5 am.
It spews everywhere
and I stand and stare,
too asleep to be real,
too real to be at rest.
So you try to slumber anyway,
only it is not working
and the green and the brown is VIBRANT
against the white of the snow.
Piled snowballs
meticulously molded for an impending battle.
When the contest begins,
you run like hell to escape the frozen fire
of balls that
grow in mass
as they fly through the air
picking up falling snow.
As they are launched
like rockets
filled with red glare,
soaring through air
in forbidden suspension,
I duck.
As your ear hits the cold hard ice,
You suddenly hear the rumble
of the fortuitous avalanche
rolling haphazardly
like puke
tossing around in the belly.
Out it comes again,
forceful regurgitation
without rhyme or reason

  Influenza
in the heat of summer vacation

and the distinct sound of a whippoorwill
in the pungently hot August night,
quietly breaking the silence
with its merciless call.

The snowball rolled flat
by the steamroller,
chafing the pavement
vaporized into the summer heat,

adding to the potency of the dank air.
I breathe distressingly,
inundated by all of the humidity.
I inadvertently perspire.
Standing exalted,
I breathe again,
in mitigation.

Total trust

I put my life in your hands
last night when I went to bed.
after what you had said,
I did not want to sleep.
I wanted to keep you safe,
alive.
I love you,
I need you,
I want you.

You promised you would be okay,
you would be here in the morning.
You would not go away,
not leave without a warning.
I held you to your word,
trusted you implicitly.
I've never trusted anyone as much as I do you.
You have never let me down.
I know with every speck of my existence,
every brain cell in my cranium,
that you would not,
lie to me.
We both know that.
you do not want to die;
Life is good.
Yet there is this piece of you
that can't keep you safe,.
that won't stop the cutting.

You succeeded tonight,
you did it,
with that contract.
That is the piece that you need to find,
come to terms with.
I don't know what it is;
you need to find the strength.
You have that special power,
you know cutting makes you feel good.
We both know that piece,
but what else can you do at that moment
to get that feeling,
that sensation

That release!
You've gone for some time
without reacting to the impulses.
Figure out why,

find out how.
Talk about the feeling of euphoria,
that makes this addiction thrive.
It is the release.
You need to replace it
with something positive,

healthy,
achievable,
successful,
loving,
nurturing,
self-respecting.

I'll help you along the way
any way that I can..
Please help yourself
before it is too late.
I do not want to watch you
disrespect yourself anymore.
Let's get help;
we both know you need it,
I need it.

Naked Man

On my way to work
one day,
out of the blue
I met a new super hero.
Sitting on the edge of a bed
was my dad
was my neighbor
was my attacker.
It is my worst nightmare-
it was Naked Man.

With what was said
in our everyday conversation
all the baggage fell
out of my vacation plane.
Yeah, I was on my honeymoon,
not dealing with the pain,
the hurt side of me,
that little girl
damaged and out of control.
Why haven't I
taken care of me lately?
Did I forget
my needs,
my worthiness,
my well being?

Smooth sailing on the open seas
of life,
and bam!
The fabric that I wear,
that strength that sits on
my shoulder
is gone,
vanished,
or at the very least
not there,
not where I can find it.
I know it's there.
The muscle has not atrophied.
It hasn't been that long
since I needed to
exercise those skills.

It's like moving
a five hundred pound barbell.
What tremendous effort it takes!

What instruments do I have?
Where are all my coping skills?
I have to tap my resources
touch base

tag home plate
find some way to be safe.
Not hurting myself.
Must nurture my wounds.

So, where do you go next
when you do not know
where your directions are?
You only know they are not
where you need them to be-
in your hand,
visible,
at your disposal.
It is a strange-familiar place,
and you're expecting to be somewhere else,
anywhere else
and fast.

I play the tapes,
test my brain,
study my notes
to try and steady myself
from my addictive behavior.
Like wanting a drink,
I feel I need it ,
deserve it.
There is lots of water in the spigot,
but I can not decide what to do next.
It is easy to use my own hands,
but I also know the secret to the Holy Grail.
It really does get better
if you take the extra time.

I don't want to fall backwards,
trip over my own feet.
I need the support of my arc-enemy,
my nemesis-
my self-mutilation.
Where are my super powers?

I need a locksmith
or someone with a jimmy.
No, I need jack.

If I can't use my hydraulic jack,
then I need to find one somewhere,
borrow one.
My super powers
aren't strong enough
to lift this weight by myself.
It is such a large burden,
so I walk,
and I talk,
and if this first person will not help me,
I'll find another,
or another,
or another.
I'll find a mirror,
Stare deep into that looking glass,
search all its dimensions.
Somewhere out there,
in there
is the secret,
the one that only I understand.
It is in there
hiding,
hidden from my memory.
I just need some help finding it.

I can do it.
I've done it before.
I was successful for a while.
I've been healthy,
Happy,

Just need to find my way.
This is just another stormy day.
In the meantime…
I am taking out my umbrella.
I will let it rain around me,
but I can stay comfortable.
I can get by,
I have the assistance
Of my totes.
And a room of friends
waiting for me inside,
drying off.

The ride of your life
(No screaming allowed)

I want to spend my life,
with you as my wife,
roller coaster or not.
I'd like to see you climb on board,
Cause right now you are riding it anyway.
You just have your eyes closed.
I want to see you open those eyes,
that heart that I am in love with.
I promise if you put your hand in mine,
squeeze it tightly,
I will hold firm,
blink my eyes like a genie,
change the scenery behind us,
and take you on a magical carpet ride.
Beautiful tapestry that glides through the sky,
higher and higher,
sunny and clear,
for our remaining years.
Occasional turbulence maybe,
Just try it.
Please do not let go.
We can ride into the sunset
on our fringed rug
Like the Love Train.

Stinkin thinkin

I need to think,
really, really think
for the first time
in a very long time.
I feel isolated,
abandoned,
speechless.
I need an outlet,
a resource,
a sparring partner,
someone to talk with.
Who will help me
sort through these feelings?
Hurting myself again,
even a little
is a huge deal
at this stage of the game.
Life
is not happy
not right this moment.
10:17 pm
Clock ticks past time.
I wonder
what to do so that I
don't lose it
altogether.
I need someone
To help me harness these thoughts,
so that I can dismiss them.
Process
things
to regain normal function.
My mind is in shambles
My heart is in pieces,
I'm like a puzzle,
I can't put the pieces
Together again.
Where did my princess go?
Why does this keep happening?
What do I do next?
I have no one,
    I don't even have myself.
Empty
uncertain

of certain pleasures
familiar to this pain
guilt
uncertainties
self-loathing
self-pity
defiance
redefined
self-hate
I didn't mean anything,
yet I don't even know
what I mean any more.
Regularly apologizing
for irregular statements
source is foggy
purple haze
smoggy thoughts
spongy processing
gray matter,
sponge saturated with words
that won't wash out
or away.
Words that seem
destined to stay.
How do I
get through today?
No where to run and hide,
yet I can't lay
by your side.
Vacillation ongoing,
You would tell me to stop,
but I can't make it
Go away.
It won't stop.
I need to go away,
far away,
for I can't process
this process
again?
Not tonight,
it is not working

Words

As we approach our anniversary,
I can't help but think
what an amazing adventure it has been.
Two glorious years of bliss
with my lady in a world
that has become far from somber.
Life is astaticism,
drenched in the perfumed rich scent
of true romance.
You make me sing and dance
playfully frolic through life
 with delight and glee.
May we forever be bonded
woman-to-woman,
wife-to-wife,
friend-to-friend.
Our love runs deep and rich,
like oil waiting to hit surface of the earth.
When the two meet
there is a powerful and prosperous flow
of excitement so strong and forceful
that if it were to hit spark
it would burn for years on end
without diminishing in strength
even ever so slightly.
May our love continue to ignite us
with passion and the genuine care
for one another's well being
and tranquility of our spirits
as we float safely together through time
in one another's arms,
with eyes opened wide
and Cheshire cat grins.

Snapshot in Time

I open my eyes and they shutter
Like the lens of a camera,
Opening and closing in quick succession,
Adjusting to the smile
That my face will soon see.

Cheerful, joyous laughter
Heard by my world,
A final reprise,
Another country heard from,
A foreign native.

Working like a seventeen-year-old,
Saving for her first car,
Demanding that this madness finds a cure,
Imagining that it sits
Right around the bend.

Like the child's parent,
That walks around a corner and disappears.
Out of mind,
Out of sight,
My eyes open once again.

This time they feel the demands
Like a hardened heart
Learning to love again,
Slowly,
Cautiously.

Never completely,
Nor without complications.
Always doubled-over,
Writhing in pain,
Waiting for that lethal blow.

You know how an avid buff
can figure out the end to a movie
Long before
The End
actually appears on screen.

The writer somehow manages to
Draw the audience in for the finale,
Anyway.

Thus am I,
At a crossroad,
Inner
-section of the mind
Awaiting the next move,
Queen to Pawn-

Change is good.

Growth is welcome.
Life should be happy
On the other side of the world.
The grass is, after all, GRIN-ER.

Or is that greener,
Wishful thinking,
The mound of clay is in your corner,
Or is it in mine?
In mind?

Transformer toy,
Resonating transmission,
Time to change clothes again,
Wild little cycle
That I ride.

Sleep dreams

Tonight you sleep
your dreams so deep
I want to lie in your arms
say, " I love you,"
kiss you everywhere
hold you tight
throughout the night
wake with exhausted lips
from all the kisses that we shared
as we rendezvous
together forever
beyond sleep
beyond morning
for life
with a wife.
It should always be fun
And never end
Hands intertwined
my love, you are
Forever on my mind

Veg-o-matic

I finally have my self-mutilating behaviors
under some realm of self-control.
No longer needing it,
still desiring it.
the urges still come.
The cravings are still there,
but I hold my own.
I dance among my chaos
laugh at this compulsion
still aching
just no longer needing the pain
simply indulging in the anarchy.
No pain,
no gain,
so I move three giant steps forward
refusing to shuffle back,
leaving footprints
in the stoical cement
of my foundation
for God to stumble across.
I feel blessed.

Survival

I feel lucky,
sometimes invincible,
like the only way I'll go
is if my own mind
puts me out of its misery.
Lost, not found,
returned to sender,
vanished without a trace.

Can't touch this,
floating above the wind.
Surviving on the wing,
of a prayer.
Oh yes, I've prayed,
 still do
 for stability.
 for safety,
 for freedom,
 For glee.

I'm coming close,
getting there.
Happier than never before.
Finding my niche.
Living on love.
Exiting the tunnel,
time traveled,
well spent,
something ventured,
understatement.
Everything gained.

 Hindsight,
 insight,
 personal growth,
 freedom,
 peace of mind,
 tranquility,
 incognito.
 Over
  it.
 With

 it.
 You are it.

 I am alive;
 I have survived

thanks to many.
Some un-adorned,
others worn,
willpower torn.
Breathing sweet fresh air.

Dream catcher

I watched you sleep tonight.
I wondered what you were dreaming.
I wish I could touch the inside of your head
with just one finger,
take a View Master glance
at what happens when you slumber.

It looks like hard work going on-
I know your mind is occupied;
I just wish I could be in there
when you are sleeping
to have fun with you
live in your dream world.

Love you at rest
just as much as I love you
when you are awake.
I want to be a part of your dreams
without pressure and stress
grow with you, as you flush your memories.

Add new ones,
travel the trail of the subconscious
together armed with commitment.
Living in love,
loving in peace,
being together, nightly in silence
hands intertwined.

Wellness Recovery Action Plan

I started WRAP as a snowflake, falling from the sky,
A pair of hands caught hold of me, told me I could fly.
They rolled me into a ball, threw me into the air,
I didn't know which way to go, it didn't seem quite fair.
I grew larger and larger, yet they wouldn't let me fall down,
They gently grabbed hold of me, placed me softly on the ground.
As I rolled, I became more confident, bigger all the while,
I climbed up the mountainside I did it with a smile.

With some HOPE and ENCOURAGEMENT, I learned to use my book,
I carried it with me and sometimes had to look.
RESPONSIBILITY was mine, as I did my personal WRAP,
I looked inside the snowball-I found an inner source to tap.
I found some resources inside of me, that I didn't know I had,
EDUCATION taught me, that growing is not so bad.
I ADVOCATED for my SELF, that became my key,
My fellow snowballs helped me, become a stronger me.

Today I set sail, without going under,
I'll never forget the group that made me sit and wonder.
Can I do this? Can I soar?
The days left me wanting, to learn a little more.
These concepts I'll share, these ideas I'll convey,
For now I am a different snowflake, then I was yesterday.
I've found a warm blanket, that will ease my chill,
The next time I need to climb that mighty, mighty hill.
So now I'll WRAP it up, and never put it down,
Tomorrow brings the secret, of the tool I have found.

A healthy way for me to cope,
A welcomed friend to offer hope
Transition made,
I am not afraid.
For I have a TOOLBOX, filled with ideas,
Not quite as overwhelming, as it first did appear.
And now I get to facilitate, lucky, lucky, me,
To share this gift of WELLNESS and my RECOVERY
Thanks to all, who held out their hands,
With soft woolen mittens, they helped me understand.

And… that is my WRAP!!

Breakdown

Everyone can help
except me.
I want to be
there
for you
to offer support
help
assistance
to show I care.

It is not
working
for us.
I try;
you cry.
I try some more,
yet no matter
how hard I do try
something just does not fit
I cannot make
it work.

Is love wrong
When you can't connect?

Only regret
try repeatedly
and now I'm sent
away.

I cannot play
you just don't want me.
Everyone else is playing
with you.

You put yourself
Down.
I hear you ridicule
yourself
come
down
hard

fall hard.
You try to be strong,
only you are not
strong
not now.

I sit and punch
keys
instead of
punching my head–
Where will this go?

Unanswered questions
solutionless
Time will tell.

Picture Perfect

For years my life was a puzzle,
meticulously crafted one individual
piece at a time.
I would construct
Pause, and build more.
nervously biting my tongue,
in deep concentration, as I worked.

Life was always tough for me.
Eventually though,
I began to have fun.
And ultimately,
I thought foolishly,
"This is it!"
I had found the last part
of my colorful conundrum.

The one that makes it,
totally perfect and faultless.
But, what I discovered instead,
was a chunk of a new puzzle.
A remarkable variation
Of the original rendering
that I had labored over.

The key
to completing every dilemma
that life tosses in your path,
is not to let the last fragment
Be the end all.
The cessation of all
that you have been striving toward.

More significantly,
it seems optimum
to commence with the final
most extraordinary
Stunning piece.
The one you undoubtedly save for last,
And put it first.
Build your world around it.

Savor its beauty,
accentuate its surroundings,
with other distinctive parts.
All assembling into

an exquisite,
and wonderfully
complicated
Self-constructed quandary.

The first shall be last and the last shall be first.
That way,
when you have finished the edifice,
you can transfer it
to canvas.
Creating a glittering
one-in-a-million
Masterpiece.

Without division
Vacant of fractures
Invisible
to the naked-eye.
Only the artist
notices the flaws.
Sees its imperfections.

To everyone else
they are labored brush strokes.
Metered processes.
Some short and swift
Others steadfast.
More rather lengthy and swirled
However, equally momentous
All part of the allure

We hold still and stare,
rarely realizing
just what the infrastructure
is truly all about.
The painter may sometimes choose to share,
her deepest secret.

That forward may really
be reverse.
That you must let go of the old
Envelop the new.
Learn from the past.
Invest in your future.
Put yourself out there.

The first shall be last and the last shall be first.

Create one gigantic representation
from 500 different pieces.
Challenge yourself
by taking steps.
It is all in the way you climb.
Many will reach the top
without falling back

But how many,
Get to do "The Rocky Dance"
At the very top of all
those mighty Art House steps?
How many can fly
with the entire Earth revolving
next to them?

The first shall be last and the last shall be first.
I am not pushing through the crowd.
I get to go hand in hand,
soar with the world around me,
Enjoying the scenery
as I travel with my newly found
Spirit.

It all starts with one piece.

Co-dependant

how do i take back something that was said?
words that pained my partners' heart,
i cannot imagine where to start,
you see, i'm also wounded from within,
i am another wayward soul,
needing her to make me whole.

how do I ingest those words of pain?
wanting to start all over again,
now my thoughts are imprisoned,
i am sorry for what was stated,
how do i tell her that i love her so?
never want to let her go.

how do i take back verbiage
when i know i have injured her sweet head,
i wish i knew where to start,
tell her i love her with all my heart,
sorry for my foolish pain,
i don't know what i thought i could gain.

how do i inhale those words of pain?
little utterance that hurt so much,
i do so wish that we could touch,
so that i could share your deep ache,
our tears are more than i can take,
can you forgive my words of thoughtlessness?

how do i retract what was said?
the quiet is more than i can stand,
i wish that i could take her soft hand,
hold her and tell her, "my darling"
that i am sorry that i am not perfect,
that i need her by my side.

how do i swallow those words of pain?
that eat at me like acid rain,
i just got so wrapped up in myself,
now my spirit screams in morbid agony,
please try to love me once again,
say you will always be my friend.
how do i refute what was said?
sorry for the poor choice of words,
i want to kiss her drowning eyes,
show you that i cannot stand to see her cry,
i need to give her one long kiss,
bring her back from the abyss.

how do i absorb the pain?
show her how much i really care,
that i am sorry she is there,
i need her here by my side,
let's not run away and hide,
our love eternal will override.

Quoting the Mighty

I want to grow upward,
not up,
not out,
wider is not an option-
upward is a factor,
a goal,
an objective.
my Holiest Communion,
Yeah, I have the cup.
I can even see it as half-full,
from where I stand now.

I just want to savor
a different flavor.
another juice,
somewhat of a shocking nectar,
shake things up,
sweet and refreshing.

I have seen the wine
on shopping lists.
in other people's grocery carts,
on movie posters,
on other faces.
I want to taste it
with my own mind,
lick my lips,
quench my ambition,
find my solace.

There is a secret world out there,
I am convinced of that.
My inspiration is that I now know,
that life can happen,
to anyone.
All you have to do is want it.
and be willing to do all the hard work.
It is all about the We
in each me
I can finally
strip in public,
undo the monster,
that has been hiding
in my closet,

My other closet.
the one that is packed.
with all of those deep,

dark secrets.

Those awful secrets,
that I must now face
To get beyond
The demons,
Poltergeists.
To unload the madness,
validate the clutter,
Throw it out.
Change my perception.

Analyze,
categorize,
rationalize
without the panic,
get past the craziness,
find my tranquility,
my pot of gold,
my main course.

Unburden the brain,
eat what has been eating at me
for all these years.
Digest,
regurgitate,
absorb the nutrients,
void the waste,
keep the wonder,
live the dream
with every waking hour.
It is possible,
salvageable,
beyond tolerable.
It is finding that piece,
that peace.

I am a work in progress,
a wayward soul
finding my direction,
following the flash of the beacon,
swimming upstream
like a trout
with strength and vigor.

Finding that sparkle,
putting things in place,
organizing the impossible,
driving the probable,
the treasures that are.

The joys in life,
the freedom to be free,
democracy of the soul,
for I want to be a whole grown-up person
no longer settling for half-assed.

Go the distance,
space traveling to a new land.
My Lady Liberty,
in God me trust.
Let's look back for the last time,
throw away what I am not using.
Downsize the unimportant,
humiliate the bad guys,
free the subservient from bondage.
Life can be tough,
But I am stronger than you know.

What a road I have ahead of me
as I grow, as I find
that I am my own elected official.
Freedom!
My ballot box is full.
The votes are being counted.
I am determined that I can do this.
I can live without monsters under my bed.
I am old enough to drink that fine wine
in my golden goblet.

Hold tight.
Dig deep.
Let loose and roar.
Chaos is in the past.

Hold my hand.
Dry my tears.
"Free at last,
Free at last,
Thank God, Almighty,
I'm free at last."
MLK

Height

I am about to have a growth spurt.
I need to ring in my year by sending out the old.
Bring in the new;
Start from scratch.

I open my eyes.
The shapes are crystal clear;
The hue so vibrant
as I FACE FRONT for the first time.

I have established my BOUNDARIES,
documented the impossible,
dominated the unlikely,
satisfied the ungrateful.

I swing from a TRAPEZE,
vacant of my safety net,
abolishing the rescue squad,
an unlucky gambler with loaded DIE.

Survival is the instinct
that I have nourished all through life.
Time to get beyond that urge,
seek out my MYSTERY DATE.

I gain momentum and delve deeper
within the pages of a Steven King NOVEL,
a heartless broken-winged bird
that has been unable to current the wind.

I hold my head high as I travel
beyond the oblivious
into the land of adulthood,
driving, thriving, OVER THE HILL.

CO-DEPENDENT no more.
indivisible,
With LIBERTY and JUSTICE
for all!

Changes

True love is caring
And not asking why
True love is sharing
our life till we die
true love is exciting
and involves letting you fly
I want to do more
Than just watch as you fly high
I want to travel with you
Way up to the sky
I want to fly away with you
It is what I would like to try
Two fluttering, fumbling spirits guided by light
Two stuttering, stumbling souls flying by night
Guided by instinct and hope while in flight
Guided by energy and a love that shines bright
Not guarded by danger this should not be a fight
But a road less traveled as we sail out of sight
Leaving our memories
How high will we go?
Sky traveling adventure
I want us to grow
I want my spirit to undergo a metamorphosis
I want you near me through all of this
Sharing the longing of the first time we kissed
Two girls together
I know we can't miss
Promise you'll take me
Spiraling gleefully into the abyss

Hands Off

I know what hands off means.
I live and breathe it.
My third life,
My would be wife
Ever-so gently,
smooth,
ever so slightly,
feel,
a softness that has left me.

I wish I understood
what she feels
that makes her scared
and reluctant

Too afraid to be caressed,
kissed gently on the neck,
the shoulders,
the oh, so lovely lips.
Why can't we have things…
the way they should be?
the way they could be?

Where did I make my mistake?
Why do I have to suffer?
Heartache,
heartbreak
no longer getting glances
of yearning,
of desire,
of passion.
It is down to money
and comfort.

Compliance.
Defiance.
Demeaning,
what does she offer
that you are not getting here?

Newness,
freshness,
desire to be with someone new
Someone to touch
Thanks so
very much
For two years
Of forever
That amounts
to nothing
now.

Headbanger

I sit and bang my head,
No security,
pain instead.
Hate to even go to bed.
Loneliness has filled my night.
Emptiness
is what I have in sight.
Bang it down upon the desk.
my heart, it hurts
miss your caress;
you know what I like the best.
Hope she fills your soul,
a tenderness that takes you out of control,
I sit wanting more;
why can't it be like before-
before you walked out the door
out of sight?
It wasn't right.
I didn't deserve what I got that day,
The day my baby moved away-
The time she went somewhere else to stay.

End of a Partnership

A part of me up and died
as I learned tonight
that she'll be the one by your side.
For a while anyway
as karma has it,
as I am learning
The oh-so-hard way
Is that it all comes back
To repeat
Over and over
again
Once more.
God is on our side;
He will be our guide,
but we each make
the journey smooth
or tumultuous.
We make our lives shake,
maybe your life will do just that
one day soon,
quake
your world may spiral downward,
I will see the pieces fall,
down once and for all.
I will not pick them up
Or even say I told you so.
Time will tell.
You will know
what this feels like,
exactly what it feels like.
I'm getting mine,
Yours may come too.
I now know it is true.
I had my share;
Now is my time,
Soon you will see
How I felt
when you left me.
Oh so happy trails
trudge lightly
and watch your step
'cause you will remember
me

when your world falls
to your feet

and the only place left to go

is down
or up.
I am choosing up.
I will go on
and you will see me from afar
in a store someday
and run the other way
while I go on to play
again.
Where did Our playground go?

It is not here,
nor will it ever be again.
Life is funny
in a bittersweet way.
see you darling
hope you find what you want
'Cause
where did that playground go?
Round and round
upside-down
topsy-turvy
It has vanished
Into thin air
Taking me prisoner
Only if I allow it.
I won't though,
I got over you
Tonight.
A tough little fight
with my shadow as
my sparing partner.
I could stay down
for the count
or choose to do battle
Again.

That is what I'm doing
My fair weather friend.
Remember the ghetto life,
Remember you were almost my wife.
My disappearing partner for life
I bid adieu

To you
We are forever through.

Munchkins

I feel like someone,
and I know who,
has taken a doughnut hole
out of my beating heart.

Not just caused pain,
or hurt,
not a break.
A real lie down and cry,
ball your eyes out,
boo boo
of significant dimension.

A penetrated hole
with the inside ripped out.
What is gone
is that little sweet spot,
that cute central circle
the filling.

With nothing in its place.
Barren remains,
Spectral
proportions,
not as insignificant,
as it may appear.

Disappeared,
fear,
got the hell out of here,
leaving me morose,
saturnine.

Not bitter,
not sweet,
centered,
in pain,
but not agony.

Look at me,
I can make it after all.
No need to **Humpty-Dumpty** fall,
found my way

Broke,
but not broken.

Downtrodden,
but not out.
I will survive.

No longer suicidal,
no longer at WAR with myself,
no longer a mess.
I can hold my own,
run with the best.

For I am no longer my very own,
best-worst enemy.
No longer scared
of my own shadow.

There is comfort here.
An Inner tranquility,
An Inner strength,
Solitude.
I am never more,
By myself.

Vagina Monologues
I feel like I am back on the roof of that building
Sitting on the edge
Deciding if I want to take that final step
To the abyss
To my dismal demise.
I am making what I hope is a conscious choice to
Save face,
Save my body from disgrace.
Not do what I yearn to do
to my very special parts,
Cut and make ruins of
That part of me that you
Made special,
Memorable.
Delighted yelling out in glee
You, my vagina and me
We were as happy as could be.
Then you walked away from me
Into the arms of someone new
Who stood outside our door
Waiting for you
To walk away
Ready to pounce
On her prey
As I sat belittled,
Insecure,
No longer happy like before.
That life of bliss
Wouldn't get another kiss.
Today I sit desperately wanting to share my secret
So you can help me sort it out.
Everyone else is ready to shout
HOSPITAL
Like that is the answer
I am searching for.
What I need
is your cure.
To stabilize and rationalize
No need to sit and patronize
Not looking for an alibi
Just want to sit and sort it out.
No reason to wonder about what might have been
Just the thought of where to begin
Again
But you won't even call
And now I just sit and
fall.

The discovery of recovery

Recovery is an adventure.
An awesome, inspiring journey,
Into forgiveness and self-acceptance.
What I have truly found
Is that the decision to get well,
And stay well comes from within.
You definitely need people
To help guide you,
The final factor
Is that you have to work at getting well.
You have to believe it is possible.

It does not come easy.
People can guide you.
Then you must show yourself,
That you want to live a healthy life.
Recovery is hard work.
It takes daily,
Hourly,
Sometimes even a single-second
At a time
Approach to success.
Recovery needs to be a ritual.

You can focus on your wellness,
Provide positive affirmation of self.
The biggest secret I have discovered,
Is that you are your own biggest asset.

You must overcome each obstacle,
By loving yourself,
Plugging along,
Each day, making it work.
Until you decide life can,
And will get better,
With your assistance.

Strive to persevere,
There can and is more to life,
Than simply existing,
There can be self-respect,
Self-worth,
Self-love,
There is so much more.
There is a healthy world
When I start to go down,

I dig in my heels
I pull upward.
I have a plan,
I have tools,
I have skills,
I have a support system.
I have myself.
I never need to be alone
Again,
I have someone upon which I can
Truly depend.
Someone to always call,
My good friend

Empty

I feel empty,
Hurt.
What did I do
But love you?
Maybe you feel
Our love was not right.
Maybe you are happy
In your new life.
Just know that you leave me empty
Unfulfilled,
Unsatisfied.
Hope you are feeling alright.
Just wanted you to know
that my heart is empty
because of you
tonight.

Sitting at the doc

Life seems good from where I sit.
I am working, I am smiling,
Yet I am a Consumer in need.
You see I still bleed,
But I hold the key to my success.
I have the ticket that won't let me regress.

I have hope,
I have strength,
I now have choices.
My heart it rejoices
No longer listening to annoying voices.

I was once a mess;
Now I am at my best.
I will stay focused.
I will discuss problems
Instead of shutting down.
I'll do what I have found

To be most significant.
I can make my own choices
Instead of letting them choose me.
I am a survivor
Not a victim
To my illness
Or my past.

Keep me in mind
As you will soon find
Other consumers
Who might be late bloomers.
I drive my recovery;
I don't dwell in the old.
I live in the now
And I am becoming quite bold.

I select the option
Of recovery,
Of Self-discovery.
My history
Is no longer a mystery.
I am proud of where I came from
I am proud of where I have gone,

But I am most blessed by the people around me
Who have made a difference that astounds me.
I am a whole person

Living life to the fullest
To my heart's content.
Life is long.
I am healthy and I am strong.
I believe in miracles.

With the right help,
The right insight,
I can now take flight
Into a world where right is right.
Help Curb the stigma,
Help stop the verbiage.
We need assistance
Not resistance.

Someone on which to rely,
Someone who will not deny
We want Normalcy;
We demand dignity.
We are your neighbors,
You colleagues,
Your family members.
We are mental health consumers
And we are everywhere.

Be patient and be kind
For what you might find
Are a lot of great people.
Who you will help mold.
Who will be touched,
And who will touch you?

Sexual Healing

My what a feeling
Has come from this healing.
No longer pain
And agony
But amazement
Wonder
Bliss.
Your kiss
Your touch
Your body
Safely with mine.
Together we go
For now we both know
That sex can be healing
If love is the feeling.

a moment of clarity

i had a moment

the best one i ever had
i realize that i am wonderful
as just me
not my past
not the omnipresent
the moment i took control
from victim
to survivor

i became powerful
not being in volatile situations
any longer
moving to the forefront
turning from inside
to out
crawling out of my Sandpit
into the here and now
the future.

it is reminiscent
of true love
it is exactly that
true love of self
worthiness
worth
positive transformation
from
half to whole
one whole
not multiple pieces.

child to woman
with one birthday
one cake
one miniscule moment
they stopped eating me
alive
it is baby alive
suckling
like a newborn

taking that first breath

can i do it?
dare i?
will i?
try?

inhale to a frightening place
arriving
crying,
dying
nevermore.

my moment of self-preservation
self-elation
a peaceful resting grounds
in which i'll dwell
the world can go to hell
because this is my lifelong-moment
50 minutes in length
a weak moment of
perpetual strength
made stronger by the muscle
of my own mind.

i pause
and realize
that you have to want to be free
in order to find justice
for one
for all
the great wall crumbles
after decades
bringing one world
to shambles
another out of shackles
the dust settles
i smile
settling never more
selecting that first slice

with icing flowers
a rose
minus the thorns
for the very first time
i am no longer blind
my life is sublime
for in this very breath-taking moment
i inhale and hold it
floating like a helium balloon
high
tickling the sky
new horizons.

Bittersweet

I once thought I'd found a treasure
Riches that I could not measure
She had beautiful green eyes and a smile to
Die for
Only my treasure changed
Or was it I who changed
I am not really clear on that exact point
I just know my green-eyed princess
Felt she had to go
To a new two-girl show
Leaving me here blind-sided
With gold-plated 18 karat of solid gold, nothing
Feeling worthless
Feeling depressed
Starting to regress
I need to grow
Create my own motion picture show
Get off my toes
Dig in my heels
Time to heal
From inside to out
Up to down
Turn that frown around
Eternity never promises
Forever
Forever, obviously doesn't mean always
Where love is concerned
It matters how life twists and turns
Blood runs deep
But love is weak
Fidelity is a structure too tall for many
Or maybe any
Bitter?
Sure.
Insecure
Always wanting to find forever
A life without that long lost treasure
Mirror, Mirror on the wall…

I look back,
yet manage to stand tall
Not letting my world fall
I will always persevere
My life, my treasure
It is quite clear

You are closer than you appear
My golden treasure deep inside of me
Forever if I let it free
It is my richest part you see
My life is wonderful
With just me
Because I make my life
My own source of glee
My own discovery of love forever
Comes in the form of loving myself
Just me
For I am myself enough
I am expensive and I am tough
Solid gold in the rough

Oxygen… after the Show

On New Years Eve 2007
Was the year I plummeted out of Heaven,
The time she left me for another.
Yet God did not leave me to falter-
Nor did He stand by and watch me fall,
He trusted me to catch myself,
As I tumbled through the sky,
Thinking again, how I would rather die.

Grab hold,
Then climb on board,
Instead of cascading over,
Landing softly in a field of clover.
Friends surrounding me,
As I brush away the dust.
All the feelings I have recovered,
That inner strength was rediscovered.

Just like 1492-
My world stopped being dismally flat,
I taught myself,
That I could bounce back.
Depression lifting-
Spirit rising,
I've found I am quite enough.
That for me, was entirely surprising.

Now New Year's Day is finally here
Wish my life was full of cheer
Who knows what lies in store,
Could it be something even more.
Optimism engulfs me-
I now finally love myself,
More than I Never imagined,
I could or would.

A forty-nine year old, feeling like 6
Finally growing up to be six-years old,
At forty-nine.
Whatever life lets be mine,
I'll savor it like the first taste-
Of sunshine,
Watching it crest out by the bay
It finally is my turn to play.

Hate is only memories that never leave,
God can help you face them,
But it is up to you to breathe,

Continued

> I inhale the new oxygen.
> Fear has gone
> What I can now clearly see
> Is what a pleasure life can be
> When you approach it
> Unencumbered and free

My New Year's Resolution

My New Year
I was told to focus on living,
Instead of just trying to survive,
Survival is good
But that decision to live,
Or the decision to pick living,
Over existing,
Is yet another step.
Damn,
I do so hate when that happens.
So what can I do
To make myself live again?

Is it again?
I think it might be for the first time,
I can't even decide.
To live means actually trying
To step outside of this very high box,
You see
Of the Three Pigs,
Mine is the brick house,
So it is my very high brick box;
That I am stepping out of.
A very solid, comfortable box,
Of which I still have some level of control.

Ah, who am I kidding?
Most of the control.
So just how do you do this living thing?
I'll step out of the house,
But what is the next move?
I don't know,
But I have come this far
Without too much going wrong,
I have learned we all have the bullshit
Almost every day.
Or some resemblance of baggage,
And lots of bills to pay.

Some people just carry it designer suitcases,
It looks pretty on the outside,
But they have soiled underwear too.
Just like me and just like you.

I carry my baggage in my lovely Wawa sack,

The one with the one-ripped-handle,
And the little tear in the plastic.
Then I cart it to and fro,
Yet, I do realize
That I have one good handle--
And that it can also be reinforced,
By holding the bag
On the bottom.

I can walk the walk;
If civilized man
Has done this living thing,
For thousands of years,
I can do an extra mile
To get to my finish line,
And then I might just
Keep on walking,
Slowly building up strength,
Endurance,
Life experiences.
Exposure,
Living conditions,

It is about time I redecorate, anyway.
It is a New Year,

525,600 minutes and all.

A New Life,
A New Chance,
I can go the distance.
I can dance around.
Why go through a picture-perfect life?
It doesn't exist ,
The way that it does
On the plasma screen.
I'll keep the bumps in between.
So I am back,
On this roller coaster ride
That is called living.
Standing with a Newborn me,

Waving at Jack, you see,
Because he knows before I do,
That I can make it,
That I can take it.

I can be a stronger me.
Happy and joyous.
Living each day,
In my own industrious way.
Never forgetting the words he taught me,
Three-years ago
Like it was today,
If you keep doing what you've always done,
You're always going to get
What you always got.

And damn it I still want something more,
This living thing I will explore ,
It can only bring a change
New adventures to endure.
But I am smarter than I ever imagined,
I breathe in and blow it out with vigor.
Not knowing for sure,
That the next breath is out there.
But, taking the chance,
That it will be,
Knowing that I can do anything,
At least once,

And I will.
Just do it!
For me,
For only me,
For the very first time,
Forever and ever,
From this point forward,
I will live life
To the best of my ability.
I will try harder than I ever have before.
I will survive and so much more,
I chose life,
I choose living.

The hell with breathing,
I want to hyperventilate,
Slide in head first!
Slowly I will catch my breath,
And exhale.

Control freak

I need control.
Ever since I was a little girl,
I could not trust
Those that were suppose to protect me.
It is difficult for me
To give up control today
Control keeps me from getting hurt,
Makes me feel like I know what is coming next.
So in a way I am entrusting you
As we grow,
To help keep me whole
Generally I cannot trust
When others take that power.
I think we both know
That soon things will change,
I just need you to know,
That i am teetering
On the edge of the ledge,
Just over the edge.
It seems kind of strange,
But change is good;
So my life will adjust,
You will find that I do indeed trust
you,
To show me the way,
To help me stay
Just one more day

Ear plugs

I was recognized today,
By my colleagues,
By my friends,
By my son,
Yet, not by myself

I could not see it,
No matter how many times
I looked at myself
In the mirror,
It was not I.

It should have been
Someone,
Anyone,
Just not me,
Not worth the recognition.

Old tapes,
Old memories,
Repeated,
The volume was deafening,
The words were precise.

They just played over,
And over some more,
Until it was time,
To change the tape

It took hours,
Fifty-minute hours,
To change the whole pile
Of worthless tape

It was replaced
With worthy tape,
What an amazing feeling
To recognize your own
Recording,
Your own voice,
And play it over and over,
For the first time

To realize,
That the music was there

All the while
Simply push the start button,

Crank it up.

Decibel after decibel,
Of fresh new music,
Screaming out,
For me to hear

Singing praise,
To the hearing-impaired
Listening, for the first time,
Proclaiming her own

Victory

Sharing with myself
Hearing it,
Believing in my abilities,
For the very first time,
In forever

Success you see,
Starts in the recordings
That you hear,
That you play,
For yourself to listen to

Absorbing positive volumes
Of diction,
Music,
With words of encouragement
Heard from the orchestra,
Resonating upward,
Inward.

Replacing the volume,
So that the newly acquired sounds,
Are all that you can hear.

From this point,
Fast forward
And replay,
Are the only controls
That can be pushed.

Cranking out good vibrations,
Successful harmonizing,
A chorus of one,
Once and for all
Beautiful music,

No longer tone deaf,
Hearing every word,
Memorizing the melody,
Striking up the band,
Aiming higher
Than ever before

Just knowing,
That the fresh harmony,
Comes from within,
And resonates outward,
Sharing with the world
My newly found friend,
Together we will make music
Until the end of life

When they carry me away
And probably then some
Dancing to its rhythm,
Enjoying the voice,
As they bellow outward,
Inside my own head

growth spurt

sun comes out
i blossom
like the morning glory
awakening from her sleep.
sun beams over
the earth.
i smile too as I open my heart
to see the new day.
you are that sun
the earth
my world
you are the center of my universe.
i revolve around you.
travel upward with you
macrocosm personified
i am you.
we stand united
hand entwined with hand
in love
in passion.
i adore you
i need you to understand
that the budding of our love
goes unchanged.
i bloom
because of you,
i thrive
when I am near you,
i strive
to be strong,
like you
proud,
powerful,
i need you to march with me
through my greatest triumph of all,
i walk
knowing that you sit on my shoulder.
dancing seductively,
i climb
noticing you are next to me,
nudging me forward
with love,

understanding you light my life,
with your fire,

tender
i want you,
need you,
by my side
for always,
beyond.
in kisses,
in health,
my princess
who turned this frog
into a beautiful woman.
who loves herself,
finally.
who lusts after you,
happily,
who wants you
near me,
for the rest of my life.

My Life

She lights my world with her smile,
She lifts my spirit with her voice,
She makes my day with that style,
I pick her over all by choice.
My dear partner that I adore,
Has such unique and genuine allure,
I can't wait to hold her near,
My sweet, my darling, my dear,
Love so special at this time,
You make my life worthwhile and fine,
May you be blessed with all the happiness you give to me.
You keep my mind willful and filled with glee.

Thump

My heart has become open,
Able to admit love,
I am so inspired by you,
With sentiments of hope,
Of future,
Of desire,
My love is so vulnerable,
You make me complete,
I love you my darling,
You are so very sweet,
I love every aspect of you,
And my love is unique,
Guided by strong forces,
I have faith it will keep.

Rebirth

The day is rainy
Dreary.
I sit here dwelling
Teary.
Why do I give it such power?
Allow it to ruin
This sweet May shower.
I am stronger now
Then I never imagined before.
Somehow.
I am a survivor.
I refuse myself to be
That stunned deer in the road.
No longer his victim,
No longer heeding a burdensome load.
Nothing can change
The things I've seen,
Some facts stay the same,
It wasn't a dream.

You see, I will still be that woman,
With frightening dreams,
I still feel his voice,
Whispering to me in between.
What seemed like so many hours
Before his bone
Filled my cheeks with their showers.
Red and dead,
I got up,
I Stammered.
After he got up,
Satisfied and Hammered.
How do you take back
Any realm of control,
When your predator
Is given the power
To Swallow you up whole?
Then Spit out tiny pieces
Of your battered soul.
Where do you go?
When home is not safe?
Where do you go?
When you don't have a place?
No sense of security,
No sense of fairness,

Home is not home,
You just feel your madness.

Your thoughts are senseless,
Your heart fills with tears.
Your life won't be life,
For so many years.
You simply exist,
You cut upon your own wrist,
You burn your body,
The rope tightly twists.
So many years later,
You sit and you cry.
Remembering the day,
Your innocence died.
Remembering the day,
That your heart first cried..
Remembering the day,
You always want to forget.
The day you remember,
That you forgot to yell.
Forever knowing,
Unable to tell.
You'll always regret,
Living through this hell.
How do you get past
That sense of victim,
Bring back that feeling of control.
That sense of power,
That tender soul.
Survival is key,
Just let it be,
Squeezed in my grasp,
Within my grip.
Let me finally
Stop biting at my lip.
Allow me to forget,
And not regret.
Just permit me to deal,
Have this not be so damn real.
Life can exist,
Without muck and mist.
My life can be,
Something I do not detest.
I'll let this go,
Put it to rest.
This life can be,
Unencumbered and free.

This life can be,
A world without portentous dark shadows,

A world of fragrant memories,
A fresh field of flowers.

So I suck in the nectar,
I spit out the seeds.
Like a bee gathering honey,
I fly through the trees.
I can live my life without fear.
I can forgive the devastation,
Of those formative years,
Forget all this anger,
Forgive all the hate,
For this is my only life,
It's got to be great.
Too many years waiting to die,
All those days through which I did cry,
For this is my time,
Life is more than half-over.
This is the time
that I hurdle into the sublime,
Above and beyond that shattered spirit.
Hovering above that captured girl,
Into a world of self-help and peace,
Into a world of solace that's soft and sweet,
A place where life is about having fun,
A life that's not over before its' begun.
Knowing that I am now safe,
Having left behind visions of that place..
Years of living in frightening space.
I can live in a world that is secure,
And still deal with these memories,
That are far from obscure.
Being joyful in the gift of giving,
Allowing myself the occasion of living.
Giving myself the joy of giving.
Elation in being just me,
Fulfilled in my life,
Not struggling to be free.
But rather finding a true sense of awareness,
Being rich with self-love and self-worth,
Allowing my needs
The right to come first
Allowing my essence, a sense of rebirth.
Forget the past.
Freedom at long last.

Copeland Treasures

What an amazing experience WRAP was.
I have so far to go, yet I feel I've come so far already.
The plan is an amazing life journey into a unique approach on wellness.
I want to share this recovery process with everyone I know.
Everyone I have yet to meet.
It covers far more than mental health issues,
Yet addresses those issues so carefully.
I have an ever-growing wrap in a newly developed lifestyle.
Health, Stability, and a safety net of sorts.
Life insurance, but it is a whole life policy.
A security blanket to WRAP myself in.
A lifejacket of sorts, to keep me afloat.
People are asking me how training went and I tell them
I was challenged, my whole being was tested, I was overwhelmed, I was amazed!
It is a wonderful concept.
It took me to my core, and I found that I liked it there.
A journey into self-recovery, self-discovery and self-awareness.
I am in tune with my inner spirit and am finding it is an awesome place to be.
Thanks for helping me to respect myself and feel like I finally have something to offer!

Thanks

It felt like I was drinking out of a broken glass.
Half-empty? Absolutely!
Never fully depleting its contents.
I drank out of that same chipped glass
for many years.
Never getting nourished
my thirst never fully-quenched.
I tried to get refreshment
finding the contents always half-empty,
.
whatever residue left-over,

once and for all.
You read ahead…

"Abandon hope, all ye who enter, here!"

You sit and you wait.
In walks a man named Jim,
Your average, ordinary, extraordinary
Crisis Specialist.
You get to talk,
He gets to listen,
Strategically you both plan,
for whatever the future might bring.
would dribble slowly,
out of the side of my mouth.

So I continued, parched
for a period of 46 years.
Until one late evening,
I SCIPped
with my broken glass
to a new place, for a drink
I think that my thirst
had gone so long unattended
that I crawled all the way there.

Like a shipwrecked soul
looking for fresh water
in a sea made of salt.

I sat in a tamper-proofed room,
Tightly squeezing my glass.

I occasionally reflect back,
and envision a Holy Grail.
A very expensive
Dollar Store
Plastic
Holy Grail.
It suddenly breaks
into fragments of color,
And I am using the shattered pieces
to reek havoc on myself.
To hide the real pain
with any other sort of ache,
anything controlled by me.
Pain incognito,
heartache,
mind-play,
heartbreak.
It is determined while you squeeze
full-blown Psychosis.

once and for all.
You read ahead…

"Abandon hope, all ye who enter, here!"

You sit and you wait.
In walks a man named Jim,
Your average, ordinary, extraordinary
Crisis Specialist.
You get to talk,
He gets to listen,
Strategically you both plan,
for whatever the future might bring.
those tiny slices of broken glass
that you get to leave this Oasis,
Time to go into the hospital,
again.
Visit number,
Ah who's counting, it's more then ten.

I find myself busy,
Acquiring new coping skills.
Locating an adhesive
I can piece my glass
together again.
Glued particles shaped into
a new configuration.
No longer a purposeful glass,
But mighty snippets of scrap glass shards.

I am left to cup my bruised-hands together
To serve as a vessel
Through which to drink
This time around,
I learn how to recycle the glass jewels
into a molded bottle.
It remains half-empty, however.
Still not fully satisfying the need
of my basic nutrients.

But there is hope,
As something foreign
Finds its' way into this metamorphosis.
The jewelry is pick up,
And placed in a new home.
Self-sufficiently I stood,
Equipped with a recycling truck,
the bottle appears half-full
for the first-time ever!
Half-------full!
I'm so excited!

Somehow this transformational process
Continues to improve.
An opportunity,
a prospect, comes into play,
Consumer inclusion!
Wellness and Recovery.

Discovery multi-hued bottle is recycled,
And it grows up,
Into a rich colorful sun-catcher.
Deep Vibrant shades
intricately placed pieces of glass
sparkling in the newly found light.
Trying to explore
a different world,
a paradise
with a palm tree and a lounge chair.
I'm there, of course,
grinning like the cat that swallowed the canary.

Holding what has become
an ice cold,
full-glass of Drenk,
neat and thirst-quenching.
Life has gone full-circle
for one-single-dollar's worth of plastic-glass.
Not only is it now filled to capacity,
It flows over.

A chilled refreshment,
cool and delicious.
 an enriched life,
a fresh perspective,
new perceptions,
a sense of Purpose.
Grasping the actual Holy Grail,
discovered
golden.
and filled to the brim,
The greatest gift one can offer
is a chance, to recycle a life
from down under.
Taking a world of tears,
into highs never imagined possible.
You perch your head up,
not ever forgetting your past,
but always
embracing your future.

You have been provided to find opportunities

You have changed lives…
Afforded myself an opportunity

for a real Life.
life of true harmony,
an expressive rainbow after a storm,
revealing a Peer dimension.
So it is boldly we go…
where no one has gone before,
Together.
By stepping up
with GIANT strides

HOT air

how do i take back something that was said?
words that pained my partners' heart,
i cannot imagine where to start,
you see, i'm also wounded from within,
i am just another wayward soul,
needing her to make me whole.

how do I ingest those words of pain?
wanting to start all over again,
now my thoughts are imprisoned,
i am sorry for what was stated,
how do i tell her that i love her so?
never want to let her go.

how do i take back verbiage
when i know i have injured her sweet head,
i wish i knew where to start,
tell her i love her with all my heart,
sorry for my foolish pain,
i don't know what i thought i could gain.

how do i inhale those words of pain?
little utterance that hurt so much,
i do so wish that we could touch,
so that i could share your deep ache,
our tears are more than i can take,
can you forgive my words of thoughtlessness?

how do i retract what was said?
the quiet is more than i can stand,
i wish that i could take her soft hand,
hold her and tell her, "my darling"
that i am sorry that i am not perfect,
that i need her by my side.

how do i swallow those words of pain?
that eat at me like acid rain,
i just got so wrapped up in myself,
now my spirit screams in morbid agony,
please try to love me once again,
say you will always be my friend.

how do i refute what was said?
sorry for the poor choice of words,

i want to kiss her drowning eyes,
show you that i cannot stand to see her cry,

i need to give her one long kiss,
bring her back from the abyss.

how do i absorb the pain?
show her how much i really care,
that i am sorry she is there,
i need her here by my side,
let's not run away and hide,
our love eternal will override.

Borderline

yesterday i lived at the border
a life of drama I am told

i bounced up and down on that border
like a trampoline i moved within its hold

i teetered along on the border
its effects definitely taking a toll

i would cross over that border
spiraling with a total loss of control

i carefully guarded my border
giving myself the job of patrol

i will always remember my border
forever part of my injured soul

living like i am forever a prisoner
destined to a life on parole

today i will venture over that border
to become a new & stronger whole

The Power of the Voice

I sometimes believe that I could fly,
Occasionally my head wants to give it a try.
I hear screams sounding much like my own,
Tugging at reality, trying to make my mind their home.
I don't need my glasses to view what is going on inside,
I see images exploding behind my own eyes.
Some call it crazy, others would say mad,
But losing your reality, it feels extremely bad.

I do know that my mind frequently cries,
As it lay in silence, staring at the sky.
I speak with other people, who struggle with this too,
We share in the drama that we each lived through.
When a person is depressed, we tell them to get out of bed,
Hard when you're imprisoned sentenced to your own head.
When I think of trauma and me as a young girl,
I envision an oyster building its pearl.

Something so valuable comes out of a shell,
While some things are more challenging, and we go through hell.
Voices screaming from everywhere as loud as they can,
Shrieking till I never want to hear my name spoken again.
The noises tap on my windows and bang on my door,
I try to open my eyes so that I can't hear them anymore.
I toss and I turn and then I cry,
As the noises they flourish and will not subside.

I try talking: to work those memories away,
Carved deep in gray matter and there they will stay.
Imbedded like fossils layered deep inside,
Expedited like tears, ripped from your eyes.
The voices continue day after day,
My demons have a neighborhood where they feel safe to play.
I try to function through all this disturbance,
And function I must, despite recurrence.

Sometimes I wonder just when things went wrong,
The answer is contained within the melody of my eternal song.

With each pivotal movement and each striking note,
I tell myself that I can still cope.
Yes, I have grown stronger than ever before,
Why am I still tormented forever more.
I've decided that trauma never goes away,
Throughout my life it is destined to stay.
It has made me into the person that I am today,
Talking with others to help clear their way.
This isn't so easy, living my life,

Consumed by one's mind, both day and night.
In case you wonder and don't share in these secrets,
Our visions continue though sometimes they weaken.
But voices bombard, they make it is all true,
They carry your scars and know how to hurt you.

A haunting of sorts goes on behind my smile,
A lifelong engraving, that chisels my style.
Pill after pill and day after day,
Will things quiet down or will they stay.
My brain inhales fresh new air, the silence so great,
My heart exhales slowly, clearing off cerebral fragments: through the poems I create.
So batten down the hatches and cover your head,
My voices are screeching all night in my bed.

All things considered, the difficulties stored,
People should such insanities never endure.
Thinking beings, should learn, NOT to hurt others,
Especially our children, our parents and lovers
I want my voices to find a new home,
I need this ruckus to leave me alone.
 So quiet down cobwebs and dust go to sleep,
I want to open my eyes and hear quiet peace.

Precious and Few

I wish you hadn't shut down the way you did last night
Putting a damper on our passion after your moment of delight

I sit here today wondering where things went wrong?
Was it bound to happen anyway? Why did you go along?

Our love was rich. Our sensuality so matched.
Yet all things soured swiftly, after you climaxed.

I know you're a wounded soldier, and I am anguished too!
I thought that we'd forgiven them, and that our love was true.

Although I know that it will never be forever out of mind,
Why did it have to flourish into that moment and hit us from behind?

I not a vicious person, yet tonight I feel like a tyrant,
Like I attacked your powerless body, without concern for your defilement.

I know you were willing and that you wanted this too,
But now I sit in judgment of the love I shared with you.

I am hoping you are safe at home and not a cutting risk,
For I have seen the depths you'll travel written on your wrist.

I pray for a phone call or even a simple text,
That will indicate you care, so we can figure out where we can go next?

Tonight I feel so empty and all my love seems in vain,
For I am deeply hurting as well, not wanting all this pain.

I hope your mind is active, processing where it all transgressed,
Last night in my delicious bed as we could not our past repress.

Daddy Long Legs

Thought about you today
Remember the day you went away
Was so sad that you went to rest
Yet somehow thought it for the best

You really stood out from the crowd
There's my Dad, I would shutter aloud
Barely admitted you were there
On most days felt like I didn't care

Wish I could have loved you just like you were
Wish our time together had been less of a blur
My dad in her pretty dress
My dad with his rather large breasts

Dad in his frilly blouse
Fluttering her way all about
Out and proud
You dressed out loud

Remember the day we went for the test?
To check for lumps in your breasts
Densely whiskered during that mammogram
You were too sick to give a damn

How I hated that very day
Being your daughter, out and gay
Watching those people as they hated you
Knowing that some of them hated me too

For the person you liked to be
Not that much different than me
You left this world on Christmas Eve
Somehow it seemed like a slight reprieve

To escape my world from your point of view
The scary truth I never knew
Never found just who you were
Woman or Man, you didn't seem quite sure

No longer a Son, No longer my Dad
It is so forever sad
To look back on your life
Knowing you couldn't get it right

A Man for years and then you would become
A Woman with breasts, her shirt undone
Parkinson's came and forever took it all away

The life you had wanted to keep at bay

Hormones no longer able to hold back
The man that was externally all but in tact
From man to woman was such a transition

Yet back to manhood without your permission

A woman standing out free and proud

It was something never quite allowed
Your life it was a transgression
A transgender indiscretion

Where was your bliss, where was your glee?
As you stood helplessly in front of me
Full of disease and really sad
That is how I remember my dear old dad

I don't remember you as strong and proud
Standing out from the crowd
More like a life of hide and seek
Barely making a tiny peep

I wish you had found happiness
Instead of just a near miss
I wish you had known who you wanted to be
If other people could only see

That you weren't that much different than me
   Just struggling to be free
A life where being different was not okay
At death you found no option to play

Did you win or did you lose?
Never allowed your right to choose
Lesbian, gay, bisexual, transgendered
The solution was never officially rendered

Today I am proud to be gay
It was not an option in your day
Thinking straight was what most people did
What did I know, Dad? I was just a kid.

On your headstone it bears the name
The you were given at birth, the one and the same
But you were two and one did not pass
And I am not sure that you are free at last

Depressive Solution

Life is good
Then bam
damn
Another down day.
Why does this reoccur?
One day voices
Next day noises
Followed by depression.

I just want to be done with all this
I teach that life is about our ups and downs
It's what makes us people
It sometimes makes us frown
I want gut-wrenching hysterical laughter
At least once
Is that seems too much to ask for?
Too much to explore
Too much for me to endure

So we talked tonight and decided that
I needed to write
That is why I am here on this awful night among nights.
Writing down my feelings
Banging out my thoughts
Keeping it real
Learning how I feel
Not focusing on my distraught
If I dwell, I'll become suicidal
Can't travel down that vicious little spiral.

Focus on the truth
That tomorrow may be brighter
My mood might get lighter
Take my meds
Go to bed
Get some rest
Wake refreshed
Why won't this go away?

I think of my friends
Keeping it real
Telling the truth
Letting them know how I feel

It does become easier to get through these glitches
If you don't dwell and get stuck
Land in a rut
Drop into the ditches.

Another bout with quicksand
Sinking
Only not going down quietly
Going down with a fight
A strength that is fierce
A desire to get out
Down to my knees
Holding on to the trees.

Pulling my way out
Swimming like a trout
Remember the strength and vigor of before
Desperately wanting to get more
Out of life
Ready for anything
Again I will fight
For a life that feels right
Give me strength
Help me see the light

Tomorrow I will awaken
Today will be in the past
This feeling will not last
My world will begin
A full mast of perpetual wind
Exploring the cause
Taking a moment to pause
Reflect…find respect

Freedom
Seeking Peace
A nuance of relief

Breathe in the air of the new day
Clean and pure
Reach for more of what life has in store
Hoping to find my own way
A serenity of sorts
A peaceful repose

Picture Perfect

For years my life was a puzzle,
Meticulously crafted one individual
Piece at a time.
I would construct,
Pause, and build more,
Nervously biting at my tongue
In deep concentration.

Life was always tough for me.
Eventually, I did begin to have fun.
And ultimately,
I thought foolishly,
"This is it!"
I had finally found the last part
of my colorful conundrum.

The one that makes it,
Totally perfect and faultless..
But what I discovered instead,
Was a chunk of a new puzzle,
A remarkable variation,
Of the original rendering,
That I had been laboring over.

The key,
To completing every dilemma
That life tosses in your path
Is not to let the last fragment
Be the end all,
The cessation of all,
That you have been striving toward.

More significantly,
It seems most optimum
To commence with the final
Most extraordinary
Part to that perplexity.
Gather it firstly,
With other significant slices,

All assembling into
An exquisite
And wonderfully
Complicated
constructed quandary.

The first shall be the last,
And the last shall be first,

That way,
When you have finished construction
You can transfer to canvas,
Creating a glittering
One-of-a-kind
Masterpiece.

Build your world around it.

Savor its beauty,
Accentuate its surroundings
With other significant slices
The first shall be last and the last shall be first,
that way,
when you are done building
you can transfer it
to canvas.
Create a gorgeous,
one-of-a-kind,
Masterpiece.

No lines
or breaks
visible
to the naked eye...
only the artist
notices the flaws,
sees its imperfections.

To everyone else
they are labored brush strokes,
measurable steps--
some short and fast,
some steadfast,
some rather long and wavy,
but each equally important,
each part of the allure.

We hold still and stare,
rarely realizing
what the infrastructure
is truly all about,
the painter may sometimes choose to share,

her deepest secret.
That forward may really
be reverse.
That you must let go of the old,
envelop the new,
learn from the past,

invest in your future,
put yourself out there.

The first shall be last and the last shall be first.
It all starts with one.
You expand,
take that stunning piece,
the one you'll
undoubtedly save for last,
 put it in first.

Create one gigantic masterpiece
from 500 pieces.
Challenge yourself
by taking steps…
It is all in the way you climb.
Many reach the top
without falling back.

But how many,
can do "The Rocky Dance"?
at the top of all
those mighty steps…
how many can fly
with the entire Earth revolving
next to them?

The first shall be last and the last shall be first.
I'm not pushing through the crowd.
I get to go hand in hand.
I get to soar with the world
All around me,
enjoying the scenery
as I travel with my new paintbrush.

Olympic Gold

Today I ran the lap to victory
With the winds of defeatism in my face
It was an uphill battle
As I struggled to keep my pace
As I passed that finish line
I often missed a step.
I never thought I'd make it
I wouldn't have placed a bet

Frequently I stumbled
Tripping over my own feet.
But instead of falling over,
I found out something neat
I regained my footing
Refocused all my sights.
I took a breath of fresh air
And followed it to light

I traveled through a land
Where life was rarely fair
Watched as others won first place
Their trophies always there
With new found strength in my possession
My survival has been great
It has taken me forever
But still it's not too late.

I have finally made my escape

And have run all my laps
I am simply delighted
To hold the secrets of the treasure maps
With my new found wisdom and my undying strength
I am forever grateful
I have overcome great lengths

Diversity and devastation
Is what I always seemed to find
My race is very focused
Yet I remained behind
Today I know what shear joy is
To hell with falling under
I can match with anyone I want
While they sit back in wonder

I finally found my own brute strength
And something else called courage

I do not feel afraid to lose
I will not be discouraged
A wellness relay is what I've won
I have found my day in the sun
From my recovery I refuse to digress
And in that I find success

I miss that guitar

Of all the things I miss so far
The part of you
I miss most is your guitar
Singing thoughts
Feeling loved
No rejection from above
I now sit
My thoughts reflect
And wonder what will happen next
I hear your songs
I see your voice
We both know
You have made a different choice

I still hear those songs
You singing out to God
Quiet audience I sat in awe
Loving you by far
I do not want you back
Yet I cannot let it go
Talent so rich and pure
It was love, in that I'm sure
So bye, bye, Ms American Pie
I'm not dwelling on the past as days go by,
I can't give it another whirl,
Your music now resonates for another girl.

The Aria of spring

Life is spectacular,
I am running and skipping home from school
on a beautiful day in May.
A splendid transformation
of my dream world.
Occasionally, I stumble across a puddle,
which I quickly soar over
with a long-running leap.
Traveling what seems more rapidly
than the rate of the wind factor.
Suddenly, stumbling upon a fragrant
array of fresh wild flowers,
colorful and vibrant.
I quickly gather them into a bunch
that is almost larger around the stems
than my big-little hand can imagine.
I squeeze tightly,
not wanting to lose
even one of my blossoms.
I want to carry them home and
offer the arrangement to my mother
so it can be place on display.
Yet, no matter how hard I try
to get my prize home,
I am either squeezing too tightly,
thus choking my rainbow of fauna,
or holding them too loosely, and they are peeling off.
Petal by petal,
one at a time.
I am noticing, too,
Because of this strange caution I exercise with this bouquet,
The bundle is wilting and starting to droop,
The tighter I embrace them,
the looser they become.
The harder I try,
the faster they fall.
So that my beautiful sidekick
grows more haggard
and weary.

Tired of my over zealous attentiveness.
I need to learn to relax and enjoy
the beauty of the moment.
Stop trying so darn hard.
Start paying attention to what I am doing-

Let things happen…
Naturally,

Let the flowers bask in the sunset of nature.
 Allow them to gently grow,
Without the intense hold
of my intervention.
Just go with the flow.
Should I stumble upon it again,
I will let them grow, as one,
with nature.
Stand back and absorb their beauty,
through study and concentration.
Not stopping and buying the print
at the gift shop.
Simply enjoying the beauty of the moment at
the museum
Innocently,
Purely,
Freshly,
Aromatically.
If you love something,
You have to know when to
let it go,
If it loves you enough,
it will come back,
Stronger.

Rebirth

The day is rainy
dreary
I sit here dwelling
Teary
Why do I allow it such power?
Allow it to ruin
This sweet May shower
I am stronger now
Then I never imagined before,
Some how
I am a survivor
I refuse myself to be
That stunned deer in the road
No longer his victim
No longer heeding a burdensome load
Nothing can change
The facts, I mean
Some things are the same
You see, I will still be that woman
With frightening dreams
I still feel his voice
Whispering to me in between
What seemed like so many hours
Before his bone
Filled my cheeks with showers
Red and dead
I got up
I Stammered
After he got up
Satisfied and Hammered
How do I take back any realm of control?
When your predator
Is given the power
To Swallow you up
Then Spit out your soul
Where do you go?
When home is not safe
Where do you go?
When you don't have enough space
No sense of security
No sense of fairness
Home is not home
You just feel the madness
Your thoughts are senseless
Your heart fills with tears

Your life won't be life
For so many years
You simply exist
You cut your own wrist
You burn your body
Your neck tightly twists
So many years later
You sit and cry
Remembering the day that innocence died
Remembering the day that your heart first did cry
Remembering the day you want to forget
The day you forgot to yell
You'll always remember being unable to tell.
You'll always regret
Living through this hell
How do you get past that sense of victim
And take back that feeling of control
That sense of power
That showered soul
Survivor is key
Just let it be
Within my grasp
Within my grip
Just let me stop
Biting my lip
Just let me forget
And not regret
Just let me deal
Let it be real
A life can exist
For me
Without muck and mist
A life can be
Something I do not detest
Let this go
Put it to rest
A life can be
Unencumbered and free
A life can be
A world without those awful dark shadows
A field of fragrant memories
A field of flowers
So I suck in the nectar
And spit out the seeds

Like a bee gathering honey I fly to the trees
I can live a life without fear
I can forgive the devastation
Of those formative years
Forget all the anger
Forgive all the hate
For this is my life
It's going to be great
Too many years waiting to die
Too many years in which I did cry
For this is the time
At a point where life is more than half over
This is the time that I hurdle
Above and beyond that captured spirit
Over and above that captured girl
Into a world of self-help and peace
Into a world of solace and sleep
To a place where life is again fun
Remembering of course that I am safe
I have left the years of frightened space
I can live in a world that is secure
And still deal with these memories
They are far from obscure
Just give myself room for living
Being happy in the gift of giving
Being happy in being just being me
Being delighted with life
Not struggling to be free
Finding a true sense of glee
And be happy with self-love and worth
Allowing my needs the right to come first
Giving my spirit a sense of rebirth

LM

the beauty and truth in a being lies in his soul,
something which can only be expressed when
he feels comfortable.
If and when you are, you speak openly,
free as the wind,
caring for no one, just yourself and the listener
as individuals.

SS

Just a quick poem to show that I care
Let's light a few candles, or send up a flare
I know this past year I have grown so much
You've helped with that and for that I am touched
I hope that you have grown in some ways too
I love our friendship and care deeply for you
My life has brought moments when I've been in doubt
You've supported my wishes and have helped sort things out
You have offered me nothing but kindness and have always shared
You've never held back and were constantly there
You're consistently sensitive when giving advice
It eases my mind and makes me think twice
This has been such a transformational year
You have been in my corner and have always stood near
Your friendship is important, you're one of a kind
Friends like you aren't easy to find
We've sent multiple emails back and forth
They've kept me on track; you've kept me on course.
You could have said I told you so with several decisions
Yet you've held back with cautious precision
Some things have been hard; I wasn't always thinking quite clear
I have made negative choices, yet still found you here
Know that I understand that you were always trying
With unconditional grace, there is no denying
You've always been patient when I have something on my mind
We go out to lunch; you help me unwind
Time will determine just what will transpire
Another approach may soon be required
Believe in yourself and you'll never lose
You can achieve anything that you yourself choose
Your choices so far seem pretty darn good
I'm learning to listen more lately; I know now that I should
It may seem like you've only been preaching to the choir
Today I'm raising my standards a little bit higher
With you in my corner, I am going to win
This is a new cycle in which to begin
This friendship has taught me so very much
I believe in myself now, I am learning to trust
Thank you so much for being a good friend
I know that you will stick with me to the dire end.

Quiet Dreams

My voices have quieted
They've all gone to sleep,
Keeping them at bay
With secrets held so deep.
Lean on one another
Together we can grow,
Count each blessing
Let others know.

That we are not crazy
Or out of our minds,
We are all people
With secrets to find.
We talk about our experience
We discuss what we hear,
But trust me these voices
They sometimes cause fear.

Most people don't understand
When voices abound,
If you share in this phenomena
I hope you have found.
Our Hearing Voices Support Group
People just like you,
Who bravely will report
When voices are breaking through.

The origin is usually trauma
Or so we are taught,
A mere part of our past
That's where we can start.
We try to help one another
Quiet the voices down,
Silencing the anguish
The flip-side profound.

We learn to control
The fragments of our past,
We learn that these voices
Don't always last.
If you are struggling
On just where to begin,
Listen to the stories
We are all in this to win.

So quiet down noises
And voices depart,
I don't need this struggle

201 Continued

Of such a heavy heart.
Life can be simple

Having peace in my mind,

Is a challenge I face often
It is what I struggle to find.
I put on my music
So I will no longer hear,
The voices inside of me
Their conflict so near.
Should they return
At the drop of a hat,
I'll turn them down quietly
You can bank on that.

Engulf my mind no longer
Get out of my head,
For I have grown stronger
Silence reigns now instead.
I know that you have all helped me
As I have battled through,
Screams of my past
This silence still seems so new

Free Falling

I always remember hearing his echo
Never knowing it would be let go
Peace and quiet is what I have found
No longer listening to those anguishing sounds

FINALLY I am free.

Replaced my fears with clearer thoughts
A new experience for which I've fought
A power I didn't know I possess
An unmeasured courage when I get stressed

I FINALLY am free.

I thought that I had achieved check long before this
Years of neglect that will not be missed
Fiercely grasping secrets from another day
And now I can stand firm and say

I am FINALLY free.

To find some solitude and leave
Hallucinations; I find slight reprieve
I take control, once and for all
I jump outward and enjoy the fall

I am free FINALLY.

Study Seminar

Time to think his voice away,
Process things another day,
Can't hold on to what doesn't work,
Years have passed and still you lurk.

You see I have voices in my head,
They torment me till I see red,
I am trying to take control,
Force my way out from his hold.

Exit clear once and for all,
Silence the voice that constantly calls,
Many years you've been on my mind,
I need a break that is mine to find.

Time to free this haunting voice,
Never knew I had the choice,
Replace his whispers with a song,
Something sweet and sing-a-long

You see I have voices in my head,
They keep me sick when I go to bed,
Scream at me throughout the night,
Keep me up; tensed and tight.

I was a victim long ago,
Yet I am still captive to my foe,
No need to linger with his voice inside,
No need to run away to hide.

Time to walk in silent peace,
Clear his voice and find relief,
The mind is a muscle that I can use,
To clear his words from my view

You see I have voices in my head,
But I can repeat positive sounds instead,
I don't have to stand by without power,
Constantly imprisoned, still I cower.

I can fight this battle through,
I don't need to keep listening to you,
When I was a child you were strong,
Forcing me to go along.

Time to live without your voice,
Comfort myself; make my choice,
If I have to listen to something repeat,

Might as well make it something sweet.

You see I have voices in my head,
But it doesn't have to be a dread,
I can make a choice to be whole,
No longer haunted, I am on parole.

I can soar through the sky,
Parachute in hand while I fly,
Free to land wherever I choose,
I have nothing left to lose.

I have my injection to see me through
Each night that I now live without you,
Voices gone, I stand enchanted,
Solace found; my roots replanted.

You see I no longer have voices in my head,
The noises are gone; the sounds are dead,
I don't have to think about that voice,
I can in the silence simply rejoice.

finding mySelf

For most of my life I wanted to die
Periodically my body would give it a good try

I never wanted to relive the pain that I had endured
Many years of therapy and they told me I would never be cured

The harder I tried to deal with my past abuse
The more it felt like there was simply no use

I tried to understand what was going on in my head
All I found were obsessive thoughts to be dead

I am the patient on which the world had given up
Talk about ironic; my heart was out of luck

I met an APN who said life could finally be good
She checked my pulse, but it didn't pummel like it should

I came to my weekly appointments and there I shared
What a difference it made to have someone who cared

The more I cleared my mind, the more powerful the voices grew
Little did I know that those delusions were an aberration of someone that I knew

Hallucinations became the norm to my abnormal thinking
Saturating my brain with overflow, like water entering a ship sinking

I learned that the voices do not have to agonize all extremes
You don't always have to succumb to the reality of the dream

Managing my voices came from within
My heart it directed me exactly where to begin

My mind is quiet now, No more voices or static
Frustrations cleared away, I no longer panic

I take what is called a long-acting injection
A medicinal potion to correct a slight imperfection

It has made my brain free of intrusion and condemnation
I now have clarity beyond my wildest expectation

I have to work hard to keep my thoughts clear
And work I have done, it's been more than a year

I am a woman with schizophrenia and on that fact I do boast
Although today I stand before as a person first and foremost

A fellow human being full of hope and aspirations
A survivor of diversity, I make a proclamation

To work hard each day and contribute to society
To never give up, life would have less variety

So be clear on this message that I bring to the table
Don't give up on any one; we may become more than just our label.

Violent Screams (rated PG) 1964-2011

Do you like it?
Like IT?
He whispers
Kissing against my ear with vile breath.
I want to scream out.
Let myself cry.
I have certainly spent time wondering why
He was ripping my skin apart.
Breaking my little heart.
Tormenting every private part.
That I had left.
That I knew better than the rest.
Brain on fire,
Body burning,
Stomach churning.
How could this happen?
How can this be?
Tears so thick I can't even see.
What in the world is happening to me?
On that hill
Making me ill.
Frozen girl.
Little girl.
Suddenly I am drifting away.
My head no longer a safe place to stay.

Tortured for daring to explore
A part of me I never knew before
Taken away from my day of fun
In a flash my world became undone
The darkness overcame the sun
Man invading my body.
Consuming me whole.
Feeling abandoned by my soul.
Voices unfold.
Do you like it?
He asks at my ear.
Do you like it, like it?
He echoes, as I burst into tears.
Like it, like it, like it!
He repeats in my mind for years.

I am desperate to be let go.
Anywhere but stuck below
This wretched child molester
My brain it starts to wane and fester
Voices are screaming from my head
Childhood innocence left for dead

Anger
Anguish
Childhood relinquished
Sanity extinguished
My mind plays a game
I hold on to the shame
Prisoner of the fire
Held by his desire
A Man-made beast
I pray to be released
Unable to leave this scene
Scars that will forever transform the pristine
Fears running deep
Interrupting the peace of my sleep
Tears flooding down my cheeks
How do I forgive?
When will I forget?
Will these voices ever cease?
Fear is eating at my brain,
He is driving me insane
Can I give up this hurt?
Become sublime.
Calm my mind.

How will I let me heal?
Do I like the way this feels?
To be held hostage day after day
Will I ever stop feeling tainted in this weird way?
Ravenously causing destruction to my core.
Till I never want to hear his voice any more.
Hate it, Hate IT!
Little girl.
Living in an unreal world
What is the price at 52?
To finally begin my life anew
For quiet, for calm
Will happiness be allowed to ensue?

Where is the solace that I wish to find?
Held captive by my own sick mind
I need to clear the way for peace,
Allow my meds time for release.
A compliant injection in my skin
Dispelling the voices experienced within
Medication that finally allows me to escape the harm
Time for those memories to be disarmed

I will change his voice!
I can make that choice!
To discover a way for the noises to depart
Find a healthy place to start.
Praying to God with all my heart
Be still this ever-screaming head
Healing
Kneeling
A positive outcome soon revealing
Rid my mind of such obtrusive thoughts
Getting help to replace these feelings

I so want to let these memories go
Clear away my wicked foe
Desperate man, sitting in the corners of my mind
In the depth of my soul
Consuming me whole.
Baby Girl,
Living life in a twisted world,
Turn-back-time,
Put my life in rewind
Learn that it wasn't fate
But instead it was hate
Teach me now before it is forever too late.

I am too old to hate myself any more
For something that happened many years before
Something I was forced to endure
I must find the key that unlocks this door.
I want out of my head
Before I go out of my mind
Before I run out of time
Prisoner at the devil's mercy
Why was he so repulsive and thirsty?
I need to find a new direction
A way to heal these imperfections
I want to get over you
Instead of keeping you over me
Get out from under you
Once and for all
I am not that small
Little girl today
I can get up and run away.
Find a new place to play
Clear my mind this disarray
Voices gone
He was wrong
I don't like IT.
I never did.
But I can face it,
Cause I am no longer a scared little kid

I choose to be free!
Take those memories away from me.
I once was blind.

But now I see.
That I have changed the voice in me
It is mine to shut off
It is mine to clear out
I am strong enough, no doubt
Like it, like IT?
Yes I do!
For I am okay, without you
I am a good person,
Brave and strong!
I have allowed you to torment my thoughts far too long.
Be gone once and for all
These are my shots to befall
I get to make the final call
Voices have vanished forever I hope
Giving me a new chance to cope.
Today is a brand new day
I hope to live the rest of my life
Without your voice in my way

Clearing a path without strife
For what has been my greatest challenge in life
Contest finally overthrown
I push you away!
Forever obliterated you will stay
I am over you!
Instead of you over me
My moment of instant gratification,
Indulgent castration.
Sanity detected
Wellness erected
Wholeness perfected
A Monumental success
Medication freeing me from my distress
Free and Clear!
Can you hear me now?
I like it!
Hear me now?
I like it a lot!
Finally I am free.
Happy to be jus' little ole me!

Sitting at the Docs

Life seems good from where I sit.
I am working. I am smiling.
Yet I am a Consumer in need.
You see I still bleed,
But I hold the key to my success.
I have the ticket that won't let me regress.
I have hope,
I have strength,
I now have choices.
My heart it rejoices
I am no longer listening to annoying voices.

I was once a mess
Now I am at my best.
I will stay focused.
I will discuss problems
Instead of shutting down
I'll do what I have found
To be most significant
I can make my own choices
Instead of letting them choose me.
I am a survivor
Not a victim
To my illness
Or my past.

Keep me in mind
As you will soon find
Other consumers
Who might be late-bloomers
I drive my wellness
I don't dwell in the old.
I live in the now
And I am becoming quite bold.
My history
Is no longer a mystery

I am proud of where I have come from
I am proud of where I have gone,
I select the option of recovery,
Of self-discovery
I am most blessed by the people around me
Who have helped make a difference that astounds me.
I am a whole person
Living life to the fullest
To my heart's content.

Life is long.
I am healthy and I am strong.

I now believe in miracles.
With the right help,
The right insight,
I can now take flight
Into a world where right is right.
Help Curb the stigma,
Help stop the verbiage.
We need assistance
Not resistance.
Someone on which to rely,
Something we do not deny
We want Normalcy
We demand dignity
We are your neighbors,
You colleagues,
Your family members, and friends
We are mental health consumers
And we are everywhere.

Be patient and be kind
For what you might find
Are a lot of great people
whom you will help
Live life to their full potential
Who can be touched
And who may touch you!

I See A Mad Moon Arising

My mind how quickly, it got so damn wet
With thoughts I am usually able to forget
Voices in the dark whispering my name
I didn't understand from whence they came.

I started to respond to the sounds that I'd hear
The conversations resulted in a panic and fear
Things had been so right, my life was just
Yet in a matter of days, I would no longer trust.

The surgery it felt like such a minor ache
My sanity was something, I was not ready to forsake
The meds the doctor prescribed to ease the pain
Quickly brought strange surroundings and a new call to shame.

I knew one night that I must be going mad
After my door and I talked for just a tad
I heard it question my inner reality
I felt it eat at my mentality.

I sat and wondered if this could be it
The point in my life where my little world no longer fit
So switching the medicine is where we began
Voices they rambled like a blowing sand.

They burned at my eyes
They made me realize
That in a split second I could simply disappear
And no one but I, would know what happened here.

An allergic reaction, quite odd indeed
One chemists' wisdom or one sick dream
Desperate to remain here on earth
With the ability to regain a sense of self-worth.

We switched the meds, one more time
A painless daze that seemed sublime
Yet in my numbed state the agony rages on
I turned the corner at the rise of the new dawn.

We switched medications again and the moon disappeared
Its' howling replaced with many new tears
 I sit in the pain and discomfort of my knee
Into a world where thoughts are now vast and free

I would rather feel pain and have it hurt
Than have my wellness continue to revert
So let it rain and let it pour

For I will wait proudly in recovery's door.

This pain will pass and you will see
A newly found peace inside of me
I stood up for my own well-being at long last
Aided by my friends, whose love is unsurpassed.

I again lose the turmoil and quiet the voices
Stand my ground and make sound choices
No pain, no gain, or so they say
I stand here humbled in some weird way.

I got help when I was in need
I saw some light while still unable to see
I followed my mind out of its' confusion
Without a trace of disillusion

The voices could have quickly gotten me lost
And taken me away at a little known cost.
I am back to square one and there I rejoice
The kryptonite no longer an option or choice

little me

i need to focus on me,
learn to care about me.
do things for me
selfish
happy
things
if i can care about myself
than i can love you.
i do for others
now
i feel i am no good
self-destructive.
i must learn to leave
that behind me
so that I can survive

Quiet Screams

My voices have quieted
They've all gone to sleep
I hold them at bay
With mysteries running deep

I lean on great friends
Together we will grow
We count our blessings
They help me to know

That I am not crazy
Or out of my mind
That we are all people
With our own secrets to find

I talk about my experience
I discuss the things that I hear
But trust me these voices
They sometimes cause fear.

Most people don't understand
When voices abound
If you share in my phenomena
I hope you have found.

A group of people who care
Folks you know you can trust
Who empower and encourage
It's an absolute must.

They respect my ideas
And bring a fresh new perspective
They offer me suggestions
Their viewpoints reflective

So where do you begin
And just whom do you select
When you need to deal with trauma
That you would much rather forget

A mere part of my past
We talk with one another
We share openly and freely
Entrusting each other

They share with me an insight
That the present should be celebrated
They give to me great foresight

That my future will be elevated

I learn to take control
Over the fragments of my past
I've learn that these voices
Don't always last

If you know someone who is struggling
On just where to begin
Send them my way
I am in this to win

I call on my team
They help me to cope
I trust them completely
They give my life hope

I can discuss all my troubles
And know that they will listen
They show me compassion
It is something I was missing

When you can talk about your life
Your achievements and ambitions
When you have a responsive audience
They don't disappear at intermission

You can share your darkest secrets
With acceptance and understanding
Obscurity clearing way
Your thoughts so demanding

The acknowledgement of you
As a fellow human being
Empowerment that is astonishing
That is what I am now seeing

So quiet down my noises
And voices depart,
I don't need to struggle
With such a heavy heart

Life can be simple
Having peace in my mind,

It is a challenge I face frequently
It is what I struggle to find

Engulf my mind no longer
Get out of my head

For now I am stronger
Silence reigns instead

My supporters have all been there
As I have battled this through
Screams of my past gone
The silence still so new

Farewell to Anna

Can you understand what it is like to have voices screaming inside your head?

You helped take that away from me, and we created a silence instead

I knew somewhere in my mind that my life was stuck

I needed you to nudge me a bit and bring me some good luck

You showed me great compassion and that became the norm

Guided me with coping skills so that a positive outlook could be formed

Our time together has passed by, but the beauty of your heart does remain

Carried deep inside of me, and that will never change

I will remember the many conversations we had, when my life was very tough

I didn't want to go on living because things had gotten pretty rough

You helped me build-up my self-worth and made living feel okay

That new found power will stay with me always, as you slowly walk away

God showered me with His love, when our two paths were crossed

A Special thanks to you from a soul whose life was all but lost

This road does part, as you will be moving on to somewhere new

I'm just grateful that our lives did touch and through it all I grew

I hope that one day this very moment will travel through your mind

And on that day you will remember that to me you are one of a kind

You will probably be helping someone else who has had about enough

By telling them it is never okay to give away your peace, no matter how tough.

Thanks,

Susanne

Suicidal Sue is what people who knew me then would say,

It made me cry inside, my screams were silent too in some weird way.

I've stopped looking at my suicide attempts as part of a fragmented past,

Today I am a different person, and I hope this awareness will always last.

I reflect on the torment that was felt when I sought my own demise,

That chaos that we battle with should never come as a total surprise.

Today my life isn't riddled with a world of sadness and tears,

I no longer wallow in bitterness and pray for my death to be near.

I have found more self-worth and courage; a wonderful inner strength,

I no longer dwell in my past and have found a sense of solace at great length.

The things that had gone wrong in my life were never all my fault,

I can now talk about those evils with people and not keep them in a vault.

People talk about battling demons like that's something that we all do,

It's the madness that I hated and feeling that my sanity was through.

I wrote about invincibility and thought I had nine lives to find,

Like the only way I would leave this life, was to be outwitted by my own mind.

I lost a friend just yesterday. She battled with mental illness and her addiction.

Her chances ran out forever. She could no longer wrestle with her affliction.

The tragedy, that surrounds sudden death, makes one feel dumbfounded.

Could I have helped them in some way? Was there a way around it?

The scary truth of the matter is that you may never know.

Was there a way to stop them? Or was it their time to go?

To me the tragedy of a life lost from mental illness and/or addiction,

Is all too real in our society and should no longer be treated with restriction.

Let's look into our brother's reddened eyes and see that he is hurting!

Let's call our mothers and daughters and stop being so disconcerting!

We all walk under the same sun and can help someone by just caring.

Our fellow human beings, our brothers and sisters whose lives we are sharing.

Mental Illness is a battle that can be won, but we should not do it all alone.

We need to look at ourselves in the mirror and learn to take it to our homes.

It is hiding in every corner; it is lurking around every bend,

Reach out and touch your neighbor, they could become a friend.

A simple kindness paid, can make all the difference in someone wanting to be alive.

Sometimes it takes a single moment shared for a person to want to survive.

DISCOMFORt

MY sPiNe SomEtimeS MisALignS

ANd NeEds To bE AdJUsTeD,

i HaVE cOmE tO acCEPt THe reALIty

    tHat I cAN nO LONgEr Be sTRaigHT.

Fortunately…

No longer needing to exhilarate

(although still aiming toward it!)

I am becoming quite happy--

and joyous

in being gay

…and finding that

whole self-discovery

refreshingly comfortable

(and slightly queer!)

At the End of the Rainbow

Drip, Drop
Splash
Splot
Washing
Cleansing
Rainingpouringsnoring
Waiting
Patient
Ly
Finally
Seeing
Being
in total awe
passionately
in
Wonder
at the power
in the vision
the finding
discovering
indulging…
in the
Flavors
that conclude
the liquid
Refreshments,
served up
by
a summer
Storm,
a mirage of color,
Dessert.

Tick, Tock,
Click,
Clock,
Passage
to a
lifetime
life
line

Sifting
Through
Garbage, Baggage,
traveling,
Finding your way
my way.
Peeking
out,
Coming
Out,
Metamorphisizing,
Homosynthesis,
a missing hue,
a missing link.
WELCOME
to the
Miraculous
Wonder-world
over,
under,
On
that
Rainbow,
a colorful
saturation
of
Diversity.

www.ingramcontent.com/pod-product-compliance
Lightning Source LLC
Chambersburg PA
CBHW081947070426
42453CB00013BA/2277